JESSE JACKSON

The African-American Biographies Series

—African-American Biographies—

JESSE JACKSON

Civil Rights Activist

Series Consultant:
Dr. Russell L. Adams, Chairman
Department of Afro-American Studies, Howard University

James Haskins

Enslow Publishers, Inc.

40 Industrial Road   PO Box 38
Box 398   Aldershot
Berkeley Heights, NJ 07922   Hants GU12 6BP
USA   UK
http://www.enslow.com

To Ann Kalkhoff

I am grateful to Kathy Benson, Lisa Crawley, Ann Kalkhoff,
Bill Rice, and Lori Wilkinson for their help.
A special thank you to Anne Jordan.

Revised edition of *I Am Somebody! A Biography of Jesse Jackson* © 1992

Library of Congress Cataloging-in-Publication Data

Haskins, James, 1941– .
    Jesse Jackson : civil rights activist / James Haskins.
      p. cm. — (African-American biographies)
    Updated ed. of: I am somebody! ©1992
    Includes bibliographical references and index.
    Summary: Presents the life, accomplishments, and goals of the civil
rights activist and politician Jesse Jackson, from his childhood in North
Carolina through his years in Chicago and Washington, D.C.
    ISBN 0-7660-1390-1
    1. Jackson, Jesse, 1941– . Juvenile literature. 2. Afro-Americans—
Biography—Juvenile literature. 3. Civil rights workers—United States—
Biography—Juvenile literature. 4. Presidential candidates—United
States—Biography—Juvenile literature. [1. Jackson, Jesse, 1941– .
2. Civil rights workers. 3. Afro-Americans—Biography.] I. Haskins, James,
1941– . I am somebody! II. Title. III. Series.
E185.97.J25 H35   2000
973.927′o92—dc21
[B]
                                                        99-043813
Printed in the United States of America

10 9 8 7 6 5 4 3 2

To Our Readers:
All Internet addresses in this book were active and appropriate when we
went to press. Any comments or suggestions can be sent by e-mail to
Comments@enslow.com or to the address on the back cover.

Illustration Credits: AP/Wide World Photos, pp. 55, 80, 112; Bill Rice,
pp. 72, 82, 97, 100; Greenville Cultural Exchange, pp. 20, 23, 25; Jesse
Jackson for President, Inc., pp. 6; Otis Hairston/North Carolina A&T
University, pp. 31, 33, 35; Photographs and Prints Division, Schomberg
Center for Research in Black Culture, The New York Public Library,
Astor, Lenox and Tilden Foundations, pp. 41; © *Washington Post*; reprint-
ed by permission of the D.C. Public Library, pp. 51, 63, 70.

Cover Photo: Courtesy the Reverend Jesse L. Jackson, Rainbow/PUSH
Coalition.

Contents

Jesse Jackson

Foreword

"I Am Somebody!"

Standing before a large enthusiastic crowd gathered from the poorest sections of Chicago, the tall, handsome young man's voice rings out, thrilling and inspiring his listeners. Their attention is riveted upon him, hope filling their eyes.

"I may be poor,
But I Am Somebody!"

His litany is seized and echoed by the crowd:

"I may be poor,
But I Am Somebody!"

With stirring and powerful oratory, Jesse Jackson became known to the black community of Chicago. His words and ideas would spread further, however—throughout the United States and across the world in the latter half of the twentieth century. By 1998, when he was considering yet a third bid for the presidency of the United States, Jesse Jackson had traveled miles and years from his beginnings. A dynamic speaker, an intelligent negotiator, a shrewd politician, and a man driven by a cause, Jesse Jackson was and is a man to be reckoned with at home and abroad. His story is the tale of a boy and a man who has become, in every sense, "Somebody!"

1

THE SOUTH AND THE STRUGGLE FOR CHANGE

From the 1940s and on into the twenty-first century, the United States has been buffeted by both social and technological change. To many who lived through these years it seemed that almost overnight every home was lit by the flickering glare of a television set, man was exploring space, and the lifestyle of Americans, once staid and predictable, was in flux. People were questioning both the values and the traditions of society and were demanding change. The most sweeping changes, however, came for black Americans, who were raising their voices in opposition to the status quo. No longer content with the secondary role society had served up to them, black Americans joined together to form the base of the civil rights movement in the 1950s and 1960s.

Although the Civil War reached an end in 1865, the onus of slavery continued long after. Black men and women were freed under the Emancipation Proclamation and the Thirteenth Amendment to the Constitution, but in reality the chains that bound them to their places in society were still as unyielding, although invisible. As John Anthony Scott wrote in *Hard Trials On My Way*:

> Slavery was sustained not alone by force but also by the power of ideas. The philosophy of slavery, which was expounded by . . . dozens of southern writers and intellectuals, taught the superiority of the white race, the inferiority of blacks, and the right of the master race to use black people, and if necessary destroy them, in the pursuit of private interest and profit.

It would take more than a law to change ingrained ideas and attitudes.

This philosophy continued to be promoted throughout the United States long after the Civil War. Despite the war and governmental decree, black men and women were not equal to white men and women; they were not fully free. With the war's end, the battle had just begun.

Reconstruction and the passage of a civil rights bill (over the veto of then-president Andrew Johnson) brought some changes to the South. But those changes were small or easily destroyed. Initially granted the right to vote, black men—and by extension, their families—met with more and more violence as they attempted to exercise that and others of their new rights. As Sidney Andrews, a white northerner who traveled throughout the South at the end of the Civil War, commented:

> . . . the whites seem wholly unable to comprehend that freedom for the Negro means the same thing as freedom for them. They readily enough admit that the Government has made him free, but appear to believe that they still have the right to exercise over him the old control. . . .

> . . . They [the newly freed black men and women] grope in the darkness of this transition period, and rarely find any sure stay for the weary arm and the fainting heart. Their souls are filled with a great, but vague longing for freedom; they battle blindly with fate and circumstance for the unseen and uncomprehended, and seem to find every man's hand raised against them. What wonder that they fill the land with restlessness!

The South was riddled with race riots, and the Ku Klux Klan and other terrorist groups gained strength in their battle to keep blacks oppressed. Throughout the turmoil, however, black men and women continued to demand their rights.

After Reconstruction many southern states and localities passed laws segregating blacks from whites. Some blacks challenged these laws. In the fall of 1870 in Louisville, Kentucky, Horace Pearce and two brothers named Robert and Samuel Fox disregarded the rules of segregation on the city's trolleys. They boarded a "whites only" car, paid their fares, and took their seats. A white passenger ordered them to leave, and when the three blacks refused, the trolley car driver called the police.

Arrested for disorderly conduct, Pearce and the Fox brothers were found guilty and fined five dollars apiece. Robert Fox would not let the matter end there. He sued the trolley car company in federal court, charging that its segregation practices violated his civil rights. He won the case and was awarded damages in the amount of fifteen dollars.

The legal victory of Robert Fox was the exception, however. By 1877, when President Rutherford B. Hayes withdrew the last northern troops from the South, the South was once again firmly under the rule of segregationists. It would be nearly eighty years before black men and women would be able to savor such a legal victory again.

The birth of the twentieth century heralded a new era—but little change. Throughout the South, signs on drinking fountains, restaurants, and restrooms proclaimed "whites only" or "colored only." Even laundries advertised, "To white trade only." Schools were rigidly segregated, and notices on trolleys and buses ordered "colored" people to sit in the rear. Most blacks resented these indignities but felt powerless to resist them.

World War II, however, spawned a new attitude among black Americans. During the war, black soldiers had fought for "their" country; now, they believed, they deserved an equal say and share in that country. They returned from the war filled with unrest and a desire to see their children raised in an atmosphere of freedom without fear. A revolution was stirring, about to be born.

During the war, progress had been made in the fight for racial equality. In the early 1940s the Congress of Racial Equality (CORE) was formed. CORE's goal was to fight for the same rights in the United States that both black and white soldiers were battling for in the European and Pacific theaters of war. It advocated "disciplined, nonviolent action," just as civil rights leaders would in the 1960s. In many ways, CORE set the format and tone of these later protests, successfully staging nonviolent sit-ins in restaurants in Chicago and other cities.

Individual recognition, also, was being given to outstanding black Americans. Not only did many blacks receive medals during the war for heroic actions but, in 1950, a black man, Dr. Ralph Bunche, was awarded the Nobel Peace Prize for his efforts toward resolving the Jewish-Arab dispute over the newly formed state of Israel. Although these steps toward equality had been taken, there was yet a long way to go before full freedom could be achieved by black men, women, and children.

Into this changing world, on October 8, 1941, a child was born, a child who, as a man, would help bring about more changes. Even at birth Jesse Jackson seemed eager to be about the business of living. The midwife who attended his delivery later commented, "It seemed that the child was in a hurry to get there. By the time the doctor arrived, I had just wrapped him in a blanket and laid him in bed with his mother." His mother, Helen Burns, named the seven-pound-four-ounce baby Jesse after his grandfather, the Reverend Jesse Robinson, founder of the Mount Emmanuel Baptist Church in Greenville, South Carolina, young Jesse's birthplace and childhood home.

2

"AIN'T
NO SUCH WORD
AS 'CAIN'T'"

reenville, South Carolina, of the 1940s was a typical, proper, "sleepy" southern town with a population of sixty-two thousand. Touted as the "textile capital of the world," it was also rigidly segregated. For the most part, black residents held the lowest-paying jobs, lived in the poorest neighborhoods, and attended all-black schools. For decades the Ku Klux Klan had cast a menacing shadow over the entire black community of Greenville, including its children, who also faced the double obstacles of inequality and poverty. In 1941 the Ku Klux Klan staged its last march through Greenville, but its presence continued to be felt long after.

That same year, Helen Burns discovered she was pregnant. Churchgoing black people in the neighborhood were shocked when she defiantly announced that she did not plan to marry. Helen was eighteen years old, a junior in high school, and very active in the Springfield Baptist Church. Pretty and personable, she had a lovely singing voice and caught the eyes of many boys her own age. She also caught the eye—and heart—of Noah Robinson, who lived next door to her family's home with his wife and three children.

Noah Robinson was a cotton grader who served as a deacon in Springfield Baptist Church. Handsome and distinguished-looking, he was also a boxing champion and semiprofessional baseball player. It is no wonder that Helen fell in love with him. There was one insurmountable obstacle to their love, however—Noah was already married.

When Helen's and Noah's relationship became public because of Helen's pregnancy, much of the black community turned its back on her. She was barred from attending her church and had to endure the gossip raging about her. Noah, for his part, openly acknowledged that he was the baby's father but did not suffer as Helen did. Because of his influence and physical prowess, many feared offending him and did not mention the incident. After Jesse's birth, Noah provided for him and visited him often when Jesse was young. Initially, Jesse did not realize that this good friend of his mother's was his father; he did not learn this until he was nine or ten years old, when his half-brother, Noah Robinson, Jr., told him. The fact that he had no legal father was common knowledge, however, and throughout his childhood, Jesse had to endure the taunts of other children, who teased him, saying he was a nobody who had no daddy.

When Jesse was two years old, Helen married Charles Henry Jackson. Charles Jackson had also grown up in Greenville and had had dreams of becoming a professional baseball player. By the age of twenty-four, Jackson realized his dream was never going to be and gave it up, becoming a postal employee and settling down with Helen and Jesse.

Charles Jackson was a good father to Jesse and formally adopted him when Jesse was sixteen. Charles tried hard to make Jesse feel he belonged. "I never told him I was not his father," recalled Charles, "because I didn't want him to grow up thinking he was different." Jesse knew, however, and despite the support and love Charles Jackson gave him, he could not help feeling a sense that something was missing in his life.

As a boy, Jesse was a bundle of energy and curiosity. A childhood friend recalled, "One thing that I remember about Jesse was his inquisitiveness. He always used to ask why. He questioned the rules at a time when everybody else had accepted them because they had always been that way." Similarly, his father, Noah Robinson, recalled that "Jesse was an unusual kind of fella, even when he was just learning to talk. He would say he was going to be a preacher. He would say, 'I'm going to lead people through the rivers of water.'"

Religion had always been important in Helen Burns's life, and when she was no longer welcome at her church, she found another. Religion became important to Jesse, also. On his father's side, Jesse came from a long line of ministers. His namesake, the Reverend Jesse Robinson, with his twin brother, Jacob, who was also a minister, had founded the Mount Emmanuel Baptist Church in Greenville, and their three brothers were ministers likewise. Charles Jackson was also a devout, churchgoing man. Each Sunday, Charles and Helen, with their two boys, Jesse and his younger brother, Charles, walked the three miles to the Long Branch Baptist Church, where Charles and Helen sang in the choir. Both Helen and Charles urged their boys to participate actively in the church and to make the church and God an intimate part of their lives.

When Jesse was nine years old, he gave his first public speech in church at a Christmas pageant. The congregation was so impressed by his devoutness and his speaking ability that he was sent to a national Sunday school convention in Charlotte, North Carolina, to represent his church. As he grew older, he became a familiar figure at Long Branch Baptist Church, presenting an oral report once each month before the congregation. Even at a young age, Jesse Jackson had accepted and made his faith an important part of his everyday life. And his faith supported him. The church encouraged him in his determination to shine and to use his abilities. The Bible, according to Jackson, "was the most important book in the house. My earliest heroes were from the Bible—David, Joseph, Samson, Paul."

Another person who supported him was his maternal grandmother, Matilda Burns, whom he called Aunt Tibby. "For God's sake, Jesse," she would tell him, "promise me you'll be somebody. Ain't no such word as 'cain't.' 'Cain't' got drowned in the soda bottle. Nothing is impossible for those who have the Lord. Come hell or high water, if you got the guts, boy, ain't nothing or nobody can turn you around." This message, which has been echoed in Jesse Jackson's own speeches later in his life, made a deep impression on him as a boy. Go for it, his grandmother told him. Find things out! Do things!

Although Aunt Tibby could neither read nor write, she knew the value of an education and encouraged Jesse to do as well as he could in school and go as far as he could. When Jesse was in elementary school, Aunt Tibby worked in the homes of a number of white people in Greenville. She kept an eye out for books and magazines that were going to be thrown out and would take them home for Jesse to read.

Aunt Tibby also taught young Jesse other lessons. "Avoid violence," she told him, and "Always be clean. Cleanliness is next to godliness." She impressed on him the need to respect others, even those who did not respect him—not an easy lesson for a boy to learn, let alone a black boy facing the racial inequalities of that time. And Jesse's first encounter with these inequalities was to come at a very young age.

Greenville, during the 1940s, was a peaceful town with no racial violence. Yet the ever-present threat of violence was felt by its black citizens. Jesse had an unconscious awareness of it; he knew his neighborhood differed from others in Greenville—and not only because of the color of its people:

> All the little homes we used to live in were owned by an old man named Mr. Hellum, who used to come around on Saturday afternoons in his little old truck to collect the rent. He was white, and he'd come around with his little book and those that didn't have the rent money would be running and hiding in the bushes and acting like they weren't home and he'd be chasing them to collect the rent. They were filled with fear and I always resented that.

Jesse's first direct experience with the threat posed by racial inequality came when he was still in elementary school. One day he went to the neighborhood store to buy some candy, as he and his friends often did. Jesse had always considered the white proprietor of the store to be his friend, but this day he found out differently. As Jesse entered the store, he discovered it was very crowded. Ignored and pushed aside by the adults, Jesse tried to get the attention of the store owner again and again. Finally, in desperation, he whistled. Suddenly, there was a dead silence in the store as all eyes turned toward the proprietor. With a look Jesse had never seen before on his face, the store owner reached under the counter, pulled out a pistol, and pointed it directly at the child. Slowly, clearly, he said, "Don't ever whistle at a white man again as long as you live." Shaking with fear and clutching his pennies, Jesse ran from the store. Even at that age, however, Jesse wondered why no one there had spoken in defense of a child.

The lesson Jesse learned, he learned well: Whites and blacks were separate and different, and blacks stayed "in their place" or else. He and his friends tried to rationalize this separation:

> We would say we didn't want to eat because we weren't hungry, or we didn't want to drink water because we weren't thirsty, or we didn't want to go to the movie theater because we didn't want to see the picture. Actually we were lying because we were afraid.

But Jesse wondered *why* things had to be this way.

There were ways for black men and women to break out of the mold cast for them by society. One was through hard work, and Aunt Tibby and Jesse's parents stressed to Jesse the value of working hard in school, in church, and in all things. Jesse was hired for his first job when he was six years old. His grandmother's friend, Mr. Summers, owned a woodyard, and he hired young Jesse to help him. Jesse's job was to pick up lumber slabs, help saw them into firewood, and then help Mr. Summers deliver them to people in the neighborhood. When not doing that, Jesse ran errands, worked on the coal truck, and raked leaves. By the time he was eleven years old and in the fourth grade, he was in charge of the woodyard, with grown men working under him, and he was also working at other jobs. When Jesse was older, he sold souvenirs and food at local football games, shined shoes, sold tickets at the local movie theater, waited on tables at a local restaurant, and caddied for golfers at the Greenville Country Club.

Throughout his childhood, Jesse applied the lessons his parents and Aunt Tibby had taught him—curiosity, determination, "stick-to-itiveness." He was intelligent, and he was not afraid of hard work. Even as a small child, Jesse Jackson was well down the road to being "somebody."

3

WIN, WIN, WIN

ome small movement toward equality for blacks in the United States came in the late 1940s and the 1950s. Under President Harry Truman, a Committee on Civil Rights was formed in 1946. In its 1947 report, the committee condemned racial prejudice and its effects and also proposed anti–poll tax and antilynching legislation, stricter enforcement of existing laws to uphold minority rights, and the establishment of a Fair Employment Practices Commission. Congress, however, acted on none of these suggestions. The first significant step in desegregation and equality was the Supreme Court ruling in the case of *Brown* v. *Topeka Board of Education* in 1954.

In *Brown* v. *Topeka Board of Education*, the Supreme Court unanimously ruled to overturn the earlier decision of *Plessy* v. *Ferguson* (1896), in which the Court had held that "separate but equal accommodations" for the races did not violate the Constitution. In the 1954 ruling, Chief

Justice Earl Warren spoke for the Court, saying that "in the field of public education the doctrine of 'separate but equal' has no place," and that separate educational facilities are "inherently unequal." A year later the Court ruled that the desegregation of schools should be done "with all deliberate speed."

The Court's decision was a direct challenge to the racially segregated southern way of life. White southerners held fast and protested. In March of 1956, a "Southern Manifesto" was issued by 96 southern congressmen denouncing the *Brown* decision and demanding "all lawful means to bring about a reversal of this decision which is contrary to the Constitution. . . ."

For black children in the South, this resistance meant that nothing changed, and for young Jesse Jackson it merely reinforced the lesson he had learned that blacks were "separate" and different. Because of the resistance to *Brown*, Jesse was forced to walk five miles to school each day. Although there was an elementary school within two blocks of his home, that school was for whites only.

The all-black Nicholtown School Jesse attended was

run-down and bleak. "There was no grass in the yard," Jesse later remembered. "I couldn't play, couldn't roll over because our school yard was full of sand. And if it rained, it turned into red dirt." Because of overcrowding, the school was forced to hold double sessions, with

Jesse's school picture when he was about twelve years old.

half the children attending in the morning and half in the afternoon. The textbooks were old and torn and scarce; the children shared books, bending together over them to read, waiting for everyone to finish before turning the pages.

Although he did well at school, Jesse had not settled into being the serious student he was later to become in high school and college. His sixth-grade teacher, Mrs. Sara Shelton, recalls:

> Like most boys, he thought school was a place to enjoy himself, to have loads of fun. I thought nothing of putting him in his place with a smack of the ruler. Sometimes his mother and I would counsel Jesse together about his thinking school was a playground.

> I used to tell him that the only chance he had to be somebody was to learn while it was easy, while he was young and had nothing else to do but learn. I always put the responsibility for being somebody on himself, telling him he had nobody to blame but himself if the world passed him by.

Despite Jesse's playfulness, Mrs. Shelton also remembers him as a hard worker and go-getter. When money was needed to get equipment for the classroom, Jesse would find ways of getting it by holding fund-raisers with his mother's help.

While still in elementary school, Jesse joined the reading club at the County Library for the Colored, reading all the books it had to satisfy his curiosity. The library was only one small room in the local community center and had few books, but it encouraged Jesse to pursue learning and showed him the many worlds and opinions that were available to him through literature.

By high school, Jesse had settled down somewhat, realizing the value of getting an education. Mrs. Norris, one of his high school teachers, remembers, "Although he received A's and B's across the board . . . I wouldn't label him a brainy person. He was ambitious and excellent through hard work."

In the ninth grade, Jesse was elected president of his class and president of the honor society, positions he continued to hold throughout high school. "Jesse was always the candidate," recalls Mrs. Norris. "Whatever office was available, Jesse would be there signing his name. He seemed to be saying 'Whether you elect me or not I'm going to run. I am the candidate.' There were plenty of people who ran against him, but usually he won. Although some kids hated his guts for always wanting to be out front, most respected him for his drive." At a place and in a time when most believed there was nowhere for blacks to go, Jesse was determined not to see life that way. He was determined he would go someplace, he would succeed.

One road to success, Jesse believed, was through sports. Jesse was a good athlete with a natural ability, and in the sixth grade he had confessed to Mrs. Shelton his dream of being a football star. "He would say it as a joke first, the way many southern boys would do, to keep people from teasing them about having ambition," said Mrs. Shelton. Behind the banter, however, Jesse was serious, and in high school, he finally got an opportunity to begin fulfilling that dream.

In 1955, Jesse entered Sterling High School, an all-black high school, and immediately signed up for football, basketball, and baseball. His size (by that time he was about six feet tall), ability, and ambition made him a star player. "He was more versatile than any [other player]," his coach, the Reverend J. D. Mathis, said. "Jesse was the kind of kid you wanted as a quarterback, clean and an all-American type. He was big and he could take a punch and then dish out a blow. I didn't worry about seeing him get up, but I'd see the opposition laying on the ground a lot of times. He was a fierce competitor."

Jesse did not neglect his studies for football, however. Mrs. Norris remembers, "He was the only football player I ever had that asked for his assignment if he was going to miss class because of football practice. The others would

Jesse (front row, center) with the Sterling High School baseball team.

make excuses." Both his parents and his coach, the Reverend Mathis, encouraged him to study, and Jesse took their encouragement to heart. As he himself would later say when speaking to young people, "Big muscles alone won't get you there, you must also know how to read and write to make it in this society."

Jesse's popularity continued throughout high school despite his busy schedule of working, sports, and studying. Noah Robinson, Jr., Jesse's half-brother who attended school with him, recalls, "All the big guys with letters would sit together at lunchtime. Jesse would be there holding court. He was like Richard Pryor, Bill Cosby and Red Foxx combined. He had the whole place cracking up."

Jesse was also popular out of school. For a time, he hung out on the streets like many black youths. On the streets, his friends called him Bo, short for Bo-Diddley. Jesse tasted street life, shooting pool and throwing dice, hanging out on the corner under a street lamp with other boys, but ultimately, he rejected it. Alluring as such an easygoing existence was, Jesse was always aware that his mother disapproved of it, and he had greater ambitions than such a life could provide, although, as he has often said since, "If it were not for the grace of God, I'd still be on the corner." Jesse had other things to do, however—better things to do.

As he had since the age of six, Jesse continued to work while in high school, using the money he earned to buy clothes at the Opportunity Shop where white people brought things for resale. Because he chose his clothes with care and bought good clothing with brand name labels, he is remembered by his teachers and fellow students as a "snappy" dresser. His concern for clothing and how he appeared sometimes brought on some teasing from other boys. "What they did not understand," says Mrs. Norris, "was that Jesse was compensating, trying to accept himself and trying to gain acceptance from others." In addition to allowing him to attain the image he desired, one of his after-school jobs led Jesse to take a closer look at the discrimination and segregation in Greenville that, until then, had always been an accepted part of his life.

Jesse was working at Claussen's Bakery in Greenville when his friend Owen Perkins, who also worked there, complained to him about the "whites only" restrooms and drinking fountains there and about the fact that the black workers were paid less than the white workers. Together, Jesse and Owen tried to organize the other black employees to protest these circumstances, but their efforts to change the bakery's policies were unsuccessful. Although their efforts failed, Jesse learned a great deal from the experience. The system didn't have to be the way it was; you could protest and, maybe, with more support, change the status quo. But change was still far in the future, and for Jesse Jackson at eighteen, the cards were still stacked against him.

This lesson was brought home to Jesse when he graduated from high school. Throughout high school,

Jesse and other students leaving Sterling High School at the end of the school day.

Jesse had continued to dream of being a professional football player. One of his chief competitors for local glory in Greenville was Dickie Dietz, the top quarterback at the all-white Greenville High School across town from Sterling High. In 1959, when both young men graduated, each was approached for recruitment by the New York Giants. It seemed to Jesse that his dream was about to come true. However, reality came crashing down on him when he discovered that while he was being offered $6,000 a year, Dietz had been offered $95,000 a year. Jesse knew Dietz was not a better player than he was—but Dietz was white. The inequities of life persisted even in the field of sports.

Angry and bitter, Jesse rejected the Giants' offer and instead accepted a football scholarship to the University of Illinois in Chicago. If he could not achieve his dream in professional football, perhaps he could become the first black quarterback to play at a Big Ten university.

As Jesse packed for college, he believed a new door was opening for him. The North was supposed to be less biased toward blacks; opportunities would exist there that could not be found in Greenville—or with the Giants. His dreams could become reality there.

4

New Beginnings

While Jesse Jackson was excelling in sports and in his studies at Sterling High School, the South was struggling with the first attempts at desegregation. The name of an obscure black minister, Dr. Martin Luther King, Jr., was starting to appear more and more frequently in both local and national newspapers.

On December 1, 1955, a small black woman named Rosa Parks took a step that would serve as a catalyst for the entire civil rights movement. On that day she boarded a city bus in Montgomery, Alabama, and took a seat in the first row of the "black" section. When a white man got on the bus and could not find a seat, the bus driver told Mrs. Parks to give up her seat to the white man. She refused. "I don't really know why I wouldn't move," she has since said. "There was no plan at all. I was just tired of giving in." Rosa Parks was arrested for breaking the Montgomery segregation ordinances.

That evening black leaders called a meeting at a local

church. It was decided there that blacks would boycott the buses to protest the arrest of Rosa Parks. When this one-day boycott was successful, they decided to extend the boycott. An organization called the Montgomery Improvement Association was formed, and a young minister named Martin Luther King, Jr., who was new in town, was elected president.

King urged the black residents of Montgomery to "walk in dignity rather than ride in shame." Compliance was strong. As Dr. King wrote in *Stride Toward Freedom*:

> I jumped in my car and for almost an hour I cruised down every major street and examined every passing bus. During this hour, at the peak of the morning traffic, I saw no more than eight Negro passengers riding the buses. By this time I was jubilant. . . . A miracle had taken place.

The black citizens of Montgomery continued to boycott the buses for more than a year, causing the bus company to lose 65 percent of its business and, as a result, causing the businesses of white merchants to suffer also. Blacks and whites were learning a lesson. As Dr. King later explained, "During the days of the Montgomery bus boycott, I came to see the power of nonviolence more and more. As I lived through the actual experience of this protest, nonviolence became more than a useful method; it became a way of life."

Finally, in November 1956, the Supreme Court ruled that bus segregation was unconstitutional, and on December 21, 1956, Dr. King and a few friends boarded a Montgomery city bus near his home and sat in the front. The first battle had been won.

The 1950s would see the escalation of this form of nonviolent protest. All over the South, blacks were starting to demand their rights.

The federal government in Washington, D.C., was beginning to pay attention. In 1957, Governor Orval Faubus of Arkansas shut down the public schools of Little Rock, Arkansas, rather than admit black students. This incident spurred Congress finally to pass a law in 1957 protecting the rights of American blacks and providing the U.S. attorney general with more power to stop interference in school desegregation. This law was buttressed by another, passed in 1960, that further protected black voting rights. Although these were not strong laws, they were a move toward change. The South was a pot on the boil—things were happening, times were changing, and black men and women were helping to bring about these changes nonviolently through boycotts, sit-ins, and marches. Young Jesse Jackson, who always liked to be in the center where things were happening, wanted to be there, too.

Jackson had gone off to college with high hopes not only of obtaining an education but also of following his dream of starring in sports; however, the University of Illinois was not as he expected. His first setback came during his initial meeting with the football coaches at Illinois. There were no black quarterbacks, they told him, and there would be no black quarterbacks. Black players were expected to fill the halfback or end positions; Jackson could not be a quarterback.

Jackson's second blow came when he faced life on the Illinois campus. Not only were black students relegated to secondary positions in sports, they were expected to assume—without complaint—secondary places on campus. For Jesse, who had always been a leader at school, this was unbearable. "We [the black students] were reduced to a subculture at Illinois," Jackson recalls. "The annual interfraternity dance was the social event of the fall, but the three black fraternities weren't invited. My black friends and I were down at the Veterans of Foreign Wars lodge listening to recordings, while the white folks were jumping live to Lionel Hampton in the gym."

The new year of 1960 did not seem to offer much to Jackson. At the University of Illinois, all he could hope for was three and a half more years of being pushed down, kept back, and stopped from excelling as his nature drove him to do. Then, suddenly, an incident in North Carolina caught his attention.

On February 1, 1960, four college students from the predominantly black Agricultural and Technical College (A&T) of North Carolina at Greensboro filed into a local Woolworth's and sat at the "whites only" lunch counter. Each ordered a cup of coffee and, when refused service, continued to sit there. Each day the students returned to sit at the lunch counter in protest, bringing their books with them and quietly studying. The owner of the store told a reporter, "They can just sit there. It's nothing to me." But after several months of the sit-in, during which students from local white colleges joined the black students, the store owner gave in, opening the lunch counter to all who wished to eat there, black or white.

Jesse Jackson, in Illinois, was electrified; revolutionary things were happening, and college students were bringing about change. He wanted to be in on it, too. At the end of his freshman year, Jackson transferred to A&T College at Greensboro and, in many ways, felt as if he were at last starting his education.

At A&T, Jackson was able to do what he had hoped to do at Illinois. He quickly distinguished himself as a quarterback and became a campus leader. As in high school, Jackson was a candidate for any office, and he was soon elected president of the student body and an officer of Omega Psi Phi fraternity. He was an honor student, and he also jumped feetfirst into the campus civil rights movement.

Another student, Jacqueline Lavinia Brown, became involved in the civil rights movement in Greensboro about the same time as Jackson; she was a freshman from Virginia, and Jackson was a sophomore.

Jacqueline had seen Jesse Jackson on campus and initially was not impressed by him. The first time they spoke, Jackson was joking with a group of other football players,

Jackson was the star quarterback on the football team at North Carolina Agricultural and Technical College.

and he shouted to Jacqueline as she passed, "Hey baby, I'm going to marry you!"

Upset, Jacqueline stepped into a mud puddle, ruining a new pair of shoes. "That put us on bad terms to start with," she recalls, "although he said he was sorry and offered to help me. But when we met later in a class we had together, I found him to be very bright and sensitive."

At the start of their relationship, Jacqueline thought Jackson was the stereotypical football player out for a good time and not interested in classes and studying, at college only for sports. As she came to know him, however, she found him to be very serious indeed. Not only did he take his classes seriously, he took everything seriously, trying to do his best in all things—including their relationship.

In 1962, Jesse and Jacqueline were married in the home of Jesse's parents in Greenville. The wedding was simple and stirring. Jacqueline's parents came from Virginia for it, and her brothers and sisters listened to the ceremony over the telephone.

The sit-ins that had been held in Greensboro had been organized by the Congress of Racial Equality (CORE). When Jackson arrived at A&T, CORE had been staging a protest or a sit-in about once a month. Jackson, full of ideas and never one to mince words, criticized their methods and pace. The other students told him to go ahead and see if he could do better—so he did.

Jackson began organizing marches and protests almost daily. Jackson would lead the way by entering a lunchroom, hotel, store, or theater and asking to be served. If service was denied, black students would immediately begin a sit-in, set up picket lines, or stage a demonstration.

In June of 1963, Jackson was arrested for the first time, on the charge of inciting a riot in downtown Greensboro. Rather melodramatically, Jackson told his fellow protesters, "I know I am going to jail. I'm going without fear. It's a principle that I have for which I'll go to jail and I'll go to the chain gang if necessary." (There were no chain gangs in North Carolina at that time.) Similarly, he told the white detective who led him away, "I'm going to jail because I refuse to let another man put a timetable on my freedom. We aren't asking for integration. We're asking for desegregation and there's a difference. I only want my freedom."

Although Jackson was not held in jail long, one person who was deeply concerned about his welfare was his young wife, Jacqueline. Just as Jesse was being released from jail, Jacqueline gave birth to their first child, their daughter Santita.

From the beginning of their married life, the young Jacksons' lives had revolved around the civil rights movement. After Santita was born, the baby was often seen at demonstrations—when Jacqueline could not find a babysitter, she carried Santita along. It was a time of excitement and change, of people helping one another for "the cause." Jacqueline remembers, "It was a time in the South when people took you in. You stayed with everybody and you shared everything." Because the Jacksons had little money and Jesse was still in school, they often lived with friends or with others who supported the civil rights movement in Greensboro.

At North Carolina A&T, Jesse Jackson continued to be a leader in student government.

Jackson's efforts in the movement were recognized his senior year at college when he was elected president of the newly formed North Carolina Intercollegiate Council on Human Rights. That same year he became more involved with the leaders of CORE and later was named field director of its southeastern operations. As a result of this involvement, Jackson attended a series of workshops on nonviolent protest led by Dr. Martin Luther King, Jr., and his staff. This was to lead Jackson to make a decision of great importance to his life.

From the time Jackson was a small child, God and the church had been an integral part of his life. Even his busy schedule at college did not cause him to neglect the church. Jacqueline remembers that, although the church was important to her also, she had stopped attending at college. Jesse got after her about this, and "after a while, I gave in and I have been going to church ever since."

Although the church was important to Jackson, he had not seriously considered making it a career. He had thought for a while that he might go into law, but even in his senior year, he had not made up his mind what he wanted to do with his life professionally. His father, Noah Robinson, remembers, however, that when Jesse was a child, he "told me he dreamed he would lead an army across the waters like Moses did. I remember telling him I don't know if you could really lead an army, but you might be a good preacher like your granddaddy was."

When Jackson arrived at A&T, his life seemed to be moving in the direction of the ministry. One night he awoke after having had a strange dream. His roommate at that time, Charles Carter, said, "He said he thought he had been called to preach. He was shaking. I never saw him look so serious before."

It was not until after he had attended the workshops on nonviolent protest and met Dr. King and his lieutenants, however, that Jackson felt sure that the decision to enter the ministry was the right one for him. Since before

Not only was he president of the student government and star quarterback on the football team, but Jackson was also an honor student and very popular with his fellow students.

the Civil War, black ministers had had a great impact on both the black and white communities in the South. The minister was an arbitrator of disputes within the black community, an advisor, and often one of the few blacks within a community who could read or write. Because of this influence, the black ministers often served as go-betweens for the white and black communities. It was only natural that black ministers such as Dr. Martin Luther King, Jr., had assumed the role of leaders in the matter of Rosa Parks and in the entire civil rights movement. They were only doing what black ministers had always done: leading their people along a path they considered right and proper and arbitrating between them and the white society.

For Jesse Jackson, the role of minister encompassed

everything he sought. Not only could he follow the church and God but he could also lead his people in the causes of equality and freedom and, he hoped, find for them and for himself better lives. As a result, in 1964, Jesse, Jacqueline, and Santita packed up and moved north to Chicago. Jackson would study at the Chicago Theological Seminary. Chicago would also be the place where, unbeknown to him in 1964, he would start on the rough road that would lead him to worldwide fame.

5

DREAMS AND REVOLUTIONS

y the end of the 1950s, many Americans were ready for a change from the placidity and the maintenance of the status quo under President Dwight D. Eisenhower. In 1960, when John Fitzgerald Kennedy entered the national political arena, some voters had welcomed him wholeheartedly. He was young, glamorous, rich, and he told Americans the things they wanted to hear: The United States was a great country, made great by its citizens. Buoyed by his idea of the "New Frontier," Americans had ushered Kennedy and his wife, Jacqueline, into the White House with royal fanfare, blessed with beneficial change—at first.

Soon after his inauguration, Kennedy began announcing plans and projects that would reinforce America's greatness. In the spring of 1961, he announced his Project Apollo, which would make the United States foremost in space. He formulated plans for the creation of what would later be known as the Peace Corps and Vista programs,

which aimed to end the world's woes through education
and unselfish effort. In 1963, he called upon Congress for
a stronger Civil Rights Act to end racial discrimination in
public facilities and employment.

Although many Americans were dazzled by Kennedy's
plans, reality was asserting itself. In April 1961, the world
image of the United States had suffered severe humilia-
tion with the Bay of Pigs invasion in Cuba and the
resulting Cuban crisis. The Soviet Union had been secret-
ly fortifying Cuba and threatened to place missiles there, a
scant hundred miles from U.S. shores. Kennedy took a
firm stance and forced the Soviets and Cuba to back off,
but America's bargaining power in the world had been
weakened. Everyone questioned how the United States
could have let such a thing happen so close to home, right
under its nose. This weakness was reinforced in August of
the same year when, despite United States protests, East
Germany closed its borders and began erection of the
Berlin Wall.

The United States was troubled at home as well. While
Congress slowly debated the proposed Civil Rights Act,
racial tension increased, with more and more sit-ins,
marches, and protests, culminating in the August 28,
1963, march on Washington in support of the bill.
Organized by Bayard Rustin, the march involved Martin
Luther King's Southern Christian Leadership Conference
(SCLC), Roy Wilkins's National Association for the
Advancement of Colored People (NAACP), James
Farmer's CORE, Whitney Young's Urban League, and
John Lewis's Student Non-Violent Coordinating
Committee, as well as religious leaders of many
denominations. The march drew the largest crowd in
Washington, D.C., history up to that time. A quarter of a
million people gathered before the Lincoln Memorial,
sharing their fears and building their dreams. One high
school student, Emily Rock, from Woodlands High School
in New York, wrote:

All around, in the faces of everyone, there was this sense of hope for the future—the belief that this march was the *big* step in the right direction. It could be heard in the voices of the people singing and seen in the way they walked. It poured out into smiles.

Hope for change was in the air and seemed to pervade all America. This idea was welcomed by many but was opposed by many, too. Then, for a moment, everything came to a halt.

On November 22, 1963, as his motorcade moved through the streets of Dallas, Texas, President John Kennedy was shot twice by Lee Harvey Oswald and killed. Two hours after Kennedy's death, Vice President Lyndon Baines Johnson was sworn in as president. As he started his term, Johnson vowed to carry out Kennedy's programs with the words, "Let us continue."

An experienced politician and wheeler-dealer, Johnson was eyed with suspicion by many of Kennedy's supporters. Yet, because of his political ties, he was able to rapidly push through Congress the Kennedy programs: a massive tax cut and the far-reaching Civil Rights Act, among others. In addition, in January of 1964, Johnson declared a multimillion-dollar "War on Poverty."

Johnson's War on Poverty met with mixed reaction. Many saw it as a reassurance that the flood of changes heralded by the Kennedy administration had not been stopped by his death, but others saw it as "too little, too late." A young seminary student in Chicago named Jesse Jackson was among those who shared the second opinion.

Jackson, as always, was busy balancing school, family, sports, and social activism while at the Chicago Theological Seminary. Classes were more difficult than he had expected, yet he tackled them with the same drive and enthusiasm with which he went at anything. As one of his professors recalled, Jackson was "a young man eager to learn everything he could as fast as he could." He also joined the seminary's basketball, baseball, and football teams, helping turn them from defeated underdogs to intermural champions against the University of Chicago. Jacqueline supported her husband's efforts, helping pay the family's expenses by working at the seminary's library and encouraging Jesse in his various activities. Jackson had also joined the Southern Christian Leadership Conference that had been founded by Dr. Martin Luther King, Jr., keeping in touch with what was occurring in the civil rights movement. "I really thought," Jackson has said, "by going to Seminary School it would be quiet and peaceful and I could reflect." The times, however, as well as Jackson's own need to strive and involve himself, were working against his attaining the peace and quiet he sought.

Bolstered by the new Civil Rights Act passed in 1964, Dr. King and the SCLC began a voter registration campaign in Selma, Alabama, in 1965. After its nonviolent protests were met with bricks, stones, and swinging police clubs, Dr. King announced his intention to stage a protest march from Selma to Montgomery, Alabama's capital. Alabama's governor, George Wallace, publicly stated that any such march would be stopped, and he called out armed state troopers. In retaliation, Dr. King urged supporters all over the United States to come to Selma and march.

With tension mounting and a confrontation between civil rights marchers and state troopers imminent, the nation's eyes turned toward Alabama. In Chicago, Jackson was excited by what was happening and felt, just as he had earlier on seeing the sit-ins in Greensboro, that he had to be there in the midst of history in the making. Dashing through the seminary halls, Jackson rounded up about half the students to accompany him to Selma to join the march. They piled into as many cars as they could get hold of and drove wildly through the night in order to reach Selma in time for the march.

As had happened after the Greensboro sit-ins, Jesse phoned home and found that he had a new baby.

While still in school, Jesse became active in the struggle for civil rights. His greatest influence was the Reverend Dr. Martin Luther King, Jr., above.

Jacqueline had given birth to his first son, Jesse Jr. Elated and relieved that both Jacqueline and his new son were fine, Jesse threw himself wholeheartedly into the Selma march, organizing people, bolstering them with heartening words.

More than fifty thousand people had responded to Dr. King's call for supporters, and President Lyndon B. Johnson had sent federal troops to protect them. Even so, Jackson and his fellow students feared there might be violence. So they all donned clerical collars—although they were not yet ordained ministers—thinking the collars might provide some protection to them. One of Jackson's professors from the seminary who was also there rebuked them for wearing the collars but did not force them to remove them. He was also aware that the collars might be helpful in avoiding bloodshed.

Dr. King himself, quiet and dignified despite the waves of hostility surrounding him, led his people from Selma to Montgomery. The march included the violence Jackson had anticipated. During the long walk, the marchers were attacked by Alabama state troopers and the watching crowds, and two white supporters were killed. The nation, seeing the brutality on its TV screens, was horrified by the savagery. In March, President Johnson called on Congress to pass a voting rights law, saying in part, ". . . what happened in Selma is part of a far larger movement which reaches into every section and state of America. It is the effort of American Negroes to secure for themselves the full blessings of American life."

Congress, however, was slow to act upon the president's request. It was not until after a summer of violence and riots in many of the major cities of the United States, capped by the riots in the Watts district of Los Angeles that caused $200 million worth of damage, that the Voting Rights Act was made into law.

During the time of the Selma march, Jackson had come to the notice of Dr. King and his staff, and at first they were irritated. Jackson was everywhere, seeming to barge in wherever King was. The SCLC leaders were especially taken by surprise when, during a number of speeches held on the steps of Brown Chapel in Selma, Jackson stood up and also spoke. Here was an unknown, inexperienced, twenty-three-year-old suddenly taking over. Yet there was something about him—Jackson was a moving speaker. The media quoted his words; the crowds listened and were swayed by him. Perhaps, thought the SCLC leaders, this young "up-start" could be of use to the movement. He was willing to work until he dropped, and he did believe deeply in what they were trying to accomplish.

When Jackson returned to Chicago, the SCLC kept an eye on him and his work, and when the civil rights movement and its leaders decided to tackle the northern cities, they remembered Jackson. And Jackson was there, ready and willing to help.

6

OPERATION
BREADBASKET

hicago was a town tightly controlled by Mayor Richard J. Daley and his political machine. Daley insisted, "We believe that we do not have segregation in Chicago. Here we recognize every man, regardless of race, national origin, or creed, and they are entitled to their rights as provided in the United States Constitution and the constitution of Illinois." But segregation, poverty, and prejudice festered in Chicago, perhaps more than in any other northern city. Since his arrival in Chicago, Jackson had been working with various groups to combat these attitudes and economic conditions. He had joined both the SCLC in Chicago and the Coordinating Council of Community Organizations (CCCO), a league of neighborhood civil rights groups led by Al Raby, a militant black schoolteacher.

After the Selma march, when Martin Luther King, Jr., and the SCLC turned their attention northward, Al Raby urged that they carry the movement to the black neighborhoods of Chicago, with their ingrained fear of Mayor Daley and his cronies. People in the overcrowded ghettos of Chicago hesitated to join any protest. Support of the Daley machine meant a continuance of grudging support from the city; going against it meant a person or group might lose housing or welfare benefits. For Jackson and other organizers, this meant waging an uphill battle to gain local support for any cause that threatened the mayor or his policies.

While Al Raby was pleading with Dr. King to come to Chicago and was organizing demonstrations and protests at city hall, Jackson was attempting to organize the black ministers of Chicago around the Chicago Freedom Movement, which was a union of the SCLC and the CCCO. It was a thankless job. Many of the ministers had ties with Daley and city hall and, at the same time, were jealous of one another's influence with both Daley and their own congregations. A number of the ministers viewed the arrival of Dr. King as a threat to their influence. Here was another minister coming in; what would he do to lessen their power? Other ministers were fearful not of losing their influence but of the city's politicians and any retribution that might fall on them if they joined the protest movement. Slowly and because of hard work, Jackson won over a majority of the ministers. One of them, the prominent Reverend Clay Evans, even took Jackson into his Fellowship Baptist Church as youth minister, a sort of apprentice minister.

In January 1966, Dr. Martin Luther King, Jr., with his staff and family, flew into Chicago. Clay Evans had furnished the car that was to pick Dr. King up, and in the driver's seat was Jesse Jackson. Although he was only one of the workers within the movement, Jackson had once again managed to advance himself, to bring himself to Dr. King's attention.

King's first rally in Chicago took place on July 11, 1966, after several months of smaller protests and speeches. It was held at Chicago's Soldier Field, and estimates of the turnout ranged from twenty-three thousand to one hundred thousand people. Regardless of the number, those who attended were enthusiastic. Later that day King led them on a march to city hall where, like his namesake, Martin Luther, who had nailed his reform demands on the door of the castle's church in Germany, King tacked forty demands on the door of city hall. These demands ranged from direct funding of Chicago's community groups by the Office of Economic Opportunity to open housing.

Mayor Daley was a wily politician, and he countered King's demands at every turn, saying, for example, that the city already had a comprehensive housing plan and that it and other programs would be in place by 1967. But Daley was nervous. King's march had included a large number of whites and threatened to erode his power at the ballot box.

King's next step in the battle with Richard Daley and the political machine included marches that were not as peaceful as his earlier marches. White residents met the marchers with rocks and bottles; Dr. King himself was hit by a rock in one such march, and, in another, Jesse Jackson was hit in the head with a brick. Black youths learned to meet these attacks in an artful manner, bringing along baseball gloves and catching the bricks and throwing them back. The police were becoming increasingly ineffectual in preventing these confrontations, and both blacks and whites were becoming angry with Mayor Daley.

The fight with city hall inadvertently came to a head in July 1966. During the first part of the month, the temperatures in Chicago had hit 100°F. The teeming ghettos sweltered under the summer sun, and children and adults fled to the streets seeking relief. One group of children turned on the fire hydrants to cool off, and when the firemen arrived to turn them off, tempers flared. Fighting and rioting filled the streets, looting was widespread, and on some rooftops, snipers crouched, firing into the crowds of police and rioters. Although Dr. King went into the streets to try to calm things down, Mayor Daley pounced triumphantly, blaming King in part for the rioting. On television, Daley said, "I think you can't directly charge it to Dr. Martin Luther King, but surely some of the people who came in here and have been talking for the last year on violence—they are on his staff. They are responsible in great measure for the instructions that have been given, for the training of these youngsters."

In August, Mayor Daley met with Dr. King and local leaders of Chicago's black communities, including Jesse Jackson. During the meetings, Daley drew up a pact, agreeing to open housing, among other things. Seeing this as a victory, Dr. King signed the pact and began to make plans to return to his home in the South, little realizing that Daley was merely making a gesture to quell dissatisfaction, that he had no intention of living up to his end of the bargain. Daley's ploy worked. In 1967, despite a massive voter registration drive in black neighborhoods, Richard Dalcy was reelected mayor with 73 percent of the votes. None of the programs he had promised to Dr. King were undertaken.

Throughout the turbulent visit of Dr. King, Jackson had not been idle. In fact, he was becoming well known in Chicago. Not only had he worked tirelessly in preparation for Dr. King's arrival, he had, during the protests and marches, been prominent on radio and television, commenting on what was happening in the city and in its black communities. Caught up in the civil rights push, however, Jackson had stopped attending his classes at the Chicago Theological Seminary, and he finally dropped out. Later, in June 1968, he was ordained a minister by the Reverend C. L. Franklin and the Reverend Clay Evans. In June of the following year, the seminary granted him an honorary degree, but in 1966, Jackson's formal schooling ended, and his future as an organizer and politician began.

When Dr. King left Chicago, he appointed Jackson to head up Operation Breadbasket for the SCLC, partially because he was the only King organizer left in Chicago. The protests and riots had crumbled many of the other organizations. Al Raby had resigned as head of the CCCO, which, without his leadership, disappeared. A number of groups believed that since an agreement had been reached with Mayor Daley in August 1966, there was no longer any need for them. This left Jackson as one of the few organizers King could count on to continue his work in Chicago.

Jackson's leadership of Operation Breadbasket, whose goal was to create jobs for blacks and help black-owned businesses, was both shrewd and successful. The goal of all businesses, Jackson knew, was to make money; threaten to take that money away, and the businesses would respond. The tool of Operation Breadbasket was the boycott. Boycotts of businesses had been successful earlier in Philadelphia under the guidance of Dr. Leon Sullivan, a black minister and member of the SCLC, and Jackson implemented them in Chicago, initially running the operation out of his own apartment.

Jackson asked the black community to do a number of things. First, he urged people to patronize black-owned businesses to keep money within the community and to encourage these businesses. Second, he called upon white-owned businesses to provide jobs for blacks and to carry products made by black companies. If a company refused, Jackson and his staff then asked the black community to join them in a boycott of that company and to form picket lines until their demands were met.

Operation Breadbasket's first success came with its boycott of Country Delight. Country Delight owned 104 stores in black neighborhoods yet had no black store employees or truck drivers. When the company refused to hire black workers at decent wages, Jackson and his staff called upon local ministers to urge their congregations to boycott the stores. Picket lines were set up at the various stores, and the pickets urged others not to shop in the stores. As the boycott began, the store owners hired men to threaten Jackson, telling him he would be killed unless he called off the boycott. Jackson ignored the threats, and three days later, Country Delight capitulated and agreed to hire forty-four black employees and begin training black drivers for its delivery trucks. The speedy success of the boycott was due, to a great extent, to the fact that Country Delight stocked many perishable goods: milk, butter, and other dairy products. As the goods on the shelves went bad, the store owners quickly gave in.

Operation Breadbasket's success with Country Delight was quickly followed by others. Jackson turned his attention to larger companies: Coca-Cola, A&P grocery stores, and Red Rooster grocery stores. Jackson's group also tackled banking. He wanted to strengthen the black-owned banks, giving them the money needed to make loans to start or improve black businesses. City officials refused Jackson's request for deposits in these banks, but the state of Illinois agreed, depositing large sums into two of the local banks.

Jackson's goal was to strengthen the community; a strong community was a proud community able to help its less fortunate members. Later, when on his own, he was to remember this idea of strength and pride. The phrase "Black is beautiful" was beginning to catch on throughout the country, and, in 1968, to reinforce this idea, Jackson organized a Black Christmas and Black Easter within Chicago's black communities. Originally the idea of Robert Lucas, a leader in the Chicago chapter of CORE, these festivals not only bolstered black pride, but they also encouraged community members to patronize local black-owned businesses. "Rather than looking through the yellow pages [for holiday shopping]," Jackson said at the time, "you've got to start looking through the black pages." Black Christmas was a big success with a huge parade of ninety floats and lots of music and was led, not by a white Santa Claus, but by a black "Soul Saint" from the South Pole. In the spring, Black Easter, with another big parade, was equally successful.

In 1971 Jackson turned his attention to staging the Black Expo, an exhibition of products made by blacks and black-owned businesses with music by black bands and art by black artists. The trade fair attracted people of all ages and gained publicity for black entrepreneurs—and for Jesse Jackson.

Jackson was becoming known as a voice of the people. This had started as early as 1966. While he was a student at the Chicago Theological Seminary, he had begun holding informal Saturday talks on civil rights with a few ministers and students. These meetings continued even after he left the seminary, and other people began to be drawn to them. They were a forum in which common problems could be discussed. By 1968 the meetings had grown too large for the seminary and were moved to the Capitol Theater on the South Side of Chicago. When Jackson was ordained, the theater became his "church" and attracted people of all ages and walks of life. Soon, Jackson was preaching regularly there, and these sermons were broadcast over the local radio. The radio stations were willing to air his sermons, believing that they were dramatic and Jackson always had something unusual to say. The Capitol Theater not only fulfilled Jackson's desire for a church but allowed him a platform from which he could inform the public of what Operation Breadbasket was doing and also express his own views. It was here that he began the chant of "I Am Somebody" that so captured his audiences and brought black pride to many Chicagoans.

While the SCLC was pleased with Jackson's efforts with Operation Breadbasket, it was uneasy about the things he was doing on his own. The SCLC was not alone. Jackson had a powerful way of speaking and moving people. Many

Jackson speaking to the southern representatives in front of "City Hall" in Resurrection City during the SCLC's Poor People's Campaign in Washington, D.C.

of his critics were wary of this strident young man who not only could capture crowds with his words but also went out and made good on the promises he made in his speeches. Where would he go from here?

Early in 1968, Jackson, with other leaders of the SCLC, had begun working with Dr. Martin Luther King, Jr., to plan a Poor People's Campaign that would include a march on Washington, D.C. The aim was to call attention to the hordes of poor and jobless people in the United States and thereby attempt to force the government to help them. Thousands flooded into Washington, building a camp, Resurrection City, next to the Lincoln Memorial and naming Jackson city manager. Dr. King, however, left the protest early, traveling to Memphis, Tennessee, with his SCLC staff to support a strike of sanitation workers. It was an opportunity, King believed, to broaden the base of the movement. Jackson accompanied King and his staff to Memphis, where, on April 4, he was to find his life, and the nation itself, suddenly, violently changed by one fatal event.

7

A DREAM DIES,
A DREAM IS BORN

hroughout his life as an activist, Dr. Martin Luther King, Jr., had faced danger. His home had been bombed; he had been jailed, stoned, and beaten; numerous threats had been made on his life. Yet because of his sincere belief in nonviolence, he had always turned the other cheek. Because of his beliefs, he not only had been recognized as the primary black American leader by two presidents, John F. Kennedy and Lyndon Baines Johnson, but also had received the Nobel Peace Prize in 1964. The downtrodden had learned that they could count on Dr. King's support in any just cause, so when the black sanitation workers of Memphis had begun their strike for a decent wage and were met with violence, they called upon Dr. King to help. He felt he could hardly refuse them.

Leaving the Poor People's Campaign in Washington, D.C., Dr. King traveled to Memphis on April 3, 1968, with a group that included young Jesse Jackson. That day they checked into the Lorraine Motel in Memphis, and later that evening, Dr. King spoke to an enthusiastic crowd at the Mason Temple. In his speech, Dr. King took the occasion to talk about the possibility of his being killed. He said, "Like anybody, I would like to live a long life. . . . But I'm not concerned about that now. . . ."

The next day, when Dr. King stepped out onto the balcony of his motel room before leaving for dinner, a group of his aides was gathered in the courtyard below him; among them was Jesse Jackson. Jackson called up to Dr. King to get his attention. He wanted to introduce Dr. King to a black musician, Ben Branch. Dr. King leaned over the balcony railing and chatted briefly with the two, then turned to go back into his room to get a jacket. As he did so, a shot rang out and a bullet struck him in the jaw, entering his neck, and severing his spinal cord. At the sound of the shot, those in the courtyard below fell to the ground, fearing the gunman would fire again. Up on the balcony, Dr. Ralph Abernathy, Dr. King's closest aide, ran to him, crying, "Oh, my God, Martin's been shot." As Abernathy cradled the dying Dr. King in his arms, chaos swirled around them. Staff members raged or collapsed with grief, and almost instantaneously it seemed, the courtyard filled with police. Hosea Williams, another staff member, recalls that "Jesse crawled up the staircase sometime after the photographers arrived . . . I can't remember him crying. He just stood there. Then I think he ran to the phone to call Coretta [Dr. King's wife]."

What ensued during the next several days both enraged and embittered other SCLC members. Suddenly Jesse Jackson was on all the news shows proclaiming that he was the last man in the world to speak to Dr. King. The story escalated to Jackson standing next to Dr. King as he was shot and Jackson, rather than Ralph Abernathy, cradling the dying Dr. King in his arms.

In the early hours of April 5, while the remaining SCLC members in Memphis were holding a meeting to

Jackson with Dr. Martin Luther King, Jr., and Dr. Ralph Abernathy on the balcony of the Lorraine Motel in Memphis, Tennessee. The day after this photograph was taken, Dr. King was assassinated.

determine their next steps, they were interrupted by someone saying, "Look who's on TV." There, on the NBC *Today Show*, bleary-eyed with fatigue and wearing a blood-stained shirt, was Jesse Jackson with his tale of Dr. King's assassination. Jackson—and the media—had named Dr. King's successor: Jesse Jackson. The SCLC was enraged by Jackson's actions, but the media seized upon Jackson's eloquence and remade history. *Time* magazine, for example, later reported that "Jackson was the last man King spoke to before he was shot in Memphis. Jackson ran to the balcony, held King's head, but it was too late." And in 1969, *Playboy* stated, "Jesse Jackson [is the] fiery heir apparent to Martin Luther King. . . . He was talking to

King on the porch of the Lorraine Motel in Memphis when the fatal shot was fired and cradled the dying man in his arms."

While the SCLC leaders sat in impotent fury, Jackson was fast moving into the role of successor to Martin Luther King, Jr. Upon Dr. King's assassination, rioting had broken out in many cities. Ironically, his death had triggered the very violence against which his whole philosophy spoke. In Chicago, street violence broke out, and Jackson was there to speak against it. Wearing the same stained shirt—stained, he claimed, with the martyr's blood of Dr. King—Jackson spoke on television to the Chicago City Council: "I am calling for nonviolence in the homes, on the streets, in the classrooms, and in our relationship to one another. I'm challenging the youth today to be nonviolent as the greatest expression of faith they can make to Dr. King—to put your rocks down, put your bottles down."

Various SCLC leaders tried to speak out against Jackson's story. Chauncey Eskridge, Dr. King's attorney, later said, "If anyone could have gotten blood on their clothes, other than Abernathy, it must have come from the balcony after King's body was removed. Jesse's appearance at Chicago's City Council with that blood on his shirt was not only deception but sacrilege. The City Council meeting offered him a public forum to be seen and heard, and that was what prompted him to appear." The voices of Jackson's detractors were faint, however, when compared to the drama, emotion, and rhetoric of the story Jackson told—and the media went for the drama rather than the truth.

In many ways Jackson's actions more than hurt SCLC leaders. Ralph Abernathy was Dr. King's second-in-command and assumed SCLC leadership on Dr. King's death. By ignoring Abernathy's place in the drama of Dr. King's assassination, Jackson was ignoring one of his own strongest supporters. King had been hesitant about hiring

Jackson as head of Operation Breadbasket in Chicago; he had believed Jackson was too young and impulsive. Abernathy, however, had spoken in Jackson's defense and persuaded Dr. King to give him a chance. Just five days before his death, Dr. King had lost patience with the young Jackson. During a meeting in Atlanta to plan action in Memphis, Jackson had been so outspoken in his opinions that he had angered King. According to a *New York Times Magazine* story, published in November of 1987, Dr. King finally left the room in disgust, and, Dr. Abernathy said:

> As we swang down the steps and turned to go down the next flight, Jesse Jackson came to the stairs and said, "Doc!" And Dr. King whirled in anger. He looked up and pointed his finger and said, "Jesse, it may be that you will carve your own individual niche in society. But don't you bother me." And Jesse was left with his mouth hanging. And we continued down the stairs.

Jackson was prepared for the new role he had suddenly assumed in the nation's eyes. Now he was, indeed, "somebody" and could wield more influence, not just locally but nationally. By the end of 1968, in addition to being a full minister, Jackson had assumed the position of national director of Operation Breadbasket, appearing on television frequently and flying around the country making speeches. He continued preaching weekly at the Capitol Theater, and it was at this time that he organized the Black Christmas and Easter and the Black Expo.

To the SCLC, Jackson was a problem. Increasingly, he was working on his own, initiating projects that did not have SCLC approval. In 1971 matters came to a head. Amid rumors that Jackson was refusing to share the profits of his Black Expo with the SCLC, Ralph Abernathy flew to Chicago to investigate. Although he determined that the charges were unfounded, Abernathy believed Jackson was doing too many things without authorization. To curb his independence, Abernathy imposed a sixty-day suspension from the SCLC on Jackson and ordered him to move to Atlanta, presumably so the SCLC could keep a closer eye on him.

Faced with this opposition and with the prospect of losing the influence he had built in Chicago, Jackson came to a decision: He would break with the SCLC and start his own organization. He no longer needed the SCLC; he was nationally recognized and had built a network in Chicago of people who trusted him and would follow him. In December 1971 he telegraphed his resignation to Ralph Abernathy, saying in part, "I pray that our goals will remain united. We must feed the hungry, clothe the naked, and set the captive free." He signed his telegram, "Jesse Jackson, Country Preacher."

A week after his resignation, with all the drama of which he is a master, Jackson held a public meeting on Chicago's South Side. Speaking before a huge portrait of Martin Luther King, Jr., Jackson announced the pending formation—on Christmas Day of 1971—of Operation PUSH (People United to Save Humanity). It would be, according to Jackson, a "rainbow coalition of blacks and whites gathered together to push for a greater share of economic and political power for all poor people in America in the spirit of Dr. Martin Luther King, Jr."

Essentially, Operation PUSH would do the same things Operation Breadbasket had done previously—work to provide economic security to minorities and minority-owned businesses. This Jackson called his "civil economics movement." There were features that differed from Operation Breadbasket, however. Operation PUSH was for all the downtrodden; although blacks were emphasized, poor whites and Hispanics were included. Operation PUSH was also to have a political program that would support candidates and legislation favorable to the poor, petition for change, and register people to vote.

With his own organization, Jackson had assumed the mantle of Martin Luther King, Jr., and, like King, had become a spokesperson for the poor and oppressed. Jesse

Jackson was now "somebody," and he was somebody who had to be heard.

Many have criticized Jesse Jackson's actions and statements following the death of Martin Luther King, Jr. Jackson, they charge, was being opportunistic, trying to seize the limelight for his own ego. Yet his critics fail to note one important factor: Jackson's deep and very genuine belief in the civil rights movement and his desire to help the less fortunate. If he bent the truth, he did so with a purpose—to carry on what Dr. King had begun.

With Dr. King's death, the civil rights movement faced extinction. King was the man who had held things together; he *was* the movement in many people's minds. Without his charismatic and forceful leadership, chaos threatened. Someone had to take his place, and Jackson, with his moving oratory and drama—and deep belief in the cause—appeared to be that someone. Dr. King had decided to go to Memphis to broaden the base of the movement. After his death, Jesse Jackson did just that with his Operation PUSH and his "Rainbow Coalition." Jackson had stepped into Dr. King's shoes, and at least to Jackson, the shoes seemed to fit.

8

PUSH AND
POLITICS

Following the death of Martin Luther King, Jr., Jackson—as always—was on the go, making speeches, involving himself in numerous projects. It seemed as if he had superhuman strength, but in December 1968 he found he did not.

That month Jackson was directing a campaign in Chicago to force construction companies to hire more black workers. With his usual zeal, he had instigated a picketing of construction sites and was himself walking a picket line in front of a building under construction when the group was arrested. In jail, he was reassuring his group and starting the procedures to get them out when, suddenly, he collapsed. Jackson was quickly rushed to a hospital, and there, doctors discovered that Jackson suffered from sickle-cell anemia.

The sickle-cell trait is common among blacks of West African descent. In Africa, this trait is a natural protection from malaria, but it can at the same time lower a person's resistance to more common diseases. With sickle-cell anemia, the red blood cells are sickle-shaped rather than round. This severely limits the cells' ability to carry oxygen and nutrients through the body, and the sickle-shaped cells can clog the blood vessels, preventing a free flow of blood.

With his usual flair for the dramatic, Jackson turned what can be a debilitating condition to his advantage, welcoming an African disease that seemed to make his ties to his roots all the closer. The disease has meant, however, that since 1968 Jackson has had to interrupt his busy schedule a number of times to be hospitalized for treatment of the anemia.

Despite his three-week illness and hospitalization, Jackson continued working as tirelessly as ever—to the dismay of the hospital staff. In December 1968 Jackson was exploring new ideas for Chicago's black communities and planning the first Black Christmas. He continued overseeing Operation Breadbasket, held press conferences in the hospital lounge, and led business meetings from his hospital bed. He realized that things could not stop merely because he was ill. And he also realized, shrewdly, the publicity value of the public seeing him in a hospital and still working for change.

Although his illness was a personal setback, Jackson was pleased to hear that the construction job campaign ended successfully. The construction union agreed to hire and train four thousand black workers.

Jackson continued to push himself, and when he started Operation PUSH in 1971, the name of his organization seemed fitting for a man with such drive. This was his own project, not one originated by others, and Jackson wanted to see it become a significant force in the nation. Working eighteen hours a day and flying thousands of miles a year, Jackson spread the ideas of PUSH throughout the country.

At first, the initials in PUSH stood for People United to Save Humanity. Later, at the suggestion of the Reverend

Alvin Pitcher, one of the ministers who participated in PUSH, the name was changed to People United to *Serve* Humanity. And PUSH did just that—through economic means.

The original civil rights movement had, in many ways, achieved its goals. Desegregation was a fact in many areas of public life. Yet there still existed a huge economic gap between most blacks and whites. Jesse Jackson's "civil economics movement" was designed to tackle this separation. As Jackson said in a 1973 article in *Ebony*, "The goal of our movement at this point in history is to secure jobs for those already working, to get the unemployed employed, and to get those working but not making a living wage organized. That has to be the three-pronged thrust of our Civil Economics Movement."

Over the years, PUSH received criticism from some arenas. Many believed the organization had not done enough for the poor and had, rather, helped those who were better off than others. A number of businesspeople— Jackson's own half-brother, Noah Ryan Robinson among them—became millionaires because of PUSH. Instead of seeing this as an indication of PUSH's success, critics saw it as favoring the less needy. As Jesse Jackson pointed out to these critics, however, a successful black business community benefited the entire community by providing money, jobs, an incentive for education, and leadership.

With Jackson working tirelessly, PUSH quickly achieved national recognition, and Jesse Jackson grew into a national figure. In 1970 he had appeared on the cover of *Time*, and by the following year was cited frequently in news articles because of both Operation PUSH and his political aspirations, for in 1971 Jesse Jackson first threw his hat into the political arena.

Operation PUSH had stressed the need for monitoring politicians and legislation in order to bring about beneficial changes for people of all races. What better way to do this, thought Jackson, than from the inside rather

At the American Enterprise Institute, Jackson spoke to a group of conservative scholars about the need for black economic self-determination.

than outside? In 1971 Jackson mounted a campaign in Chicago against Mayor Richard J. Daley, forming a third party, the Bread 'N Butter Party.

Jackson's campaign against Daley had a threefold purpose: to get blacks to register to vote, to get independents on the ballot, and to get a genuine representation of blacks in local government by defeating Daley's political machine. There were blacks on Daley's city council but they were referred to as "house-boys" because they went along with what Daley wanted and were mere token representatives of the black people in Chicago. But Jackson's campaign was doomed from the start.

As had so often happened in the past—and would happen in the future—Jackson made the announcement that he would run for mayor without first consulting local black leaders. Many were angry that they had not been asked for their advice and support, and they turned their backs on Jackson.

Jackson was also up against Chicago's system. For an independent candidate to get onto the ballot, that candidate had to circulate petitions. These petitions then had to be submitted to Daley's own certification program for verification. In other words, to run against Mayor Daley, one had to get his approval. In an attempt to circumvent Daley's control, Jackson took his petitions through the courts, all the way to the Supreme Court. However, he was defeated; he was unable to get the Court to declare Daley's certification system unconstitutional.

While the battle to get on the ballot was being waged, Jackson was both gaining and losing support. Dr. Ralph Abernathy, putting aside any enmity he might have felt against Jackson after Dr. King's death, publicly endorsed him as a good alternative to the traditional party candidates. Jackson, however, kept wavering as to whether he would really run or not, and as a result, many people began to take him and his campaign less seriously. His campaign seemed disorganized and confused.

In 1971 Richard Daley won the election handily; Jackson lost by a wide margin. Jackson, however, having had a taste of politics and realizing the instrument of change that a politician could be, now made the decision to involve himself—and PUSH—even more actively in politics. In 1972 he proposed the organization of a Liberation Party with the purpose of nominating a black presidential candidate. Unfortunately, because his credibility had been weakened in his 1971 mayoral campaign, his proposal was not taken seriously by those to whom he looked for support. He was successful, however, in another area of politics. With Chicago attorney William Singer, he managed to prevent Mayor Daley and the Cook County Democratic organization from being seated at the

Democratic National Convention by exposing violations of the party rules for delegate selection by Mayor Daley.

While Jackson was involving himself and Operation PUSH in politics, he was not ignoring other areas. His Saturday morning sermons continued. The Capitol Theater had been leased by Operation Breadbasket, so Operation PUSH bought a large, drafty former Jewish synagogue on Chicago's South Side and renamed it Dr. King's Workshop. From its stage, Jackson, sporting a huge Afro, dashiki, and medallions, as was the fashion at the time for blacks, would emotionally urge his followers to be "somebody" each Saturday. Because he was a dramatic and now politically controversial figure, Jackson's Saturday sermons were regularly carried on local television as well as radio.

In addition to preaching, Jackson continued to organize and oversee PUSH's campaign against discrimination by large businesses. One early protest against General Foods, for example, resulted in General Foods' agreeing to hire hundreds of minority workers, use black lawyers and doctors when special consultants were needed, place $20 million of its insurance with black insurance companies, and deposit money into black banks. Other large corporations, such as Ford Motor Company, Burger King, and Kentucky Fried Chicken, were acceding to PUSH's demands.

By 1973, although Jackson had suffered some setbacks politically, PUSH seemed well established as a major vehicle of economic change in the United States. Perhaps Jackson's proudest personal moment came that year on October 6, when his hometown of Greenville, South Carolina, held a weekend-long festival in his honor. Finally, here in the town where he had grown up and where, as a child, he had been refused admittance to movie theaters and restaurants, Jackson was returning as a hero.

The *Greenville-Piedmont News* proclaimed, "Here

Comes the Son," and hotels and restaurants put up signs welcoming Jackson home. There was even a homemade sign hung up by his boyhood friends: "Hey, Bo-Diddley." To Jackson, Greenville's welcome was a demonstration of how effective the civil rights movement had been—and it was also a declaration that he had, indeed, become "somebody." He was no longer an anonymous, illegitimate black child in a poor section of town. To underscore his sense of belonging, he and Jacqueline later purchased his boyhood home in Greenville.

While personally gratified, however, Jackson used the occasion to stress the work of PUSH. As he said in his speech at a banquet held in his honor at Greenville's Jack Tar Poinsett Hotel (where he himself had waited tables as a youth), "My point used to be personal, now it is public. I used to preach for reputation. Now I preach for edification." And what did he wish to edify his listeners about?—that "we must open up the doors of a nation to the masses of the poor." People throughout the country, both black and white, were going hungry and dying of hunger. Both voters and politicians had to tackle these problems and bring hope to the world.

As 1973 ended, Jackson appeared to be a rising star, and no one and nothing could get in his way. He seemed to be on a roll that could not be stopped.

9

TRY
HARDER

lthough 1973 ended on a high note, 1974, for Jesse Jackson and the nation as a whole, was a year of reversals and setbacks. The Watergate scandal had tarnished the image of the office of the president and of the government in general, culminating on August 5, 1974, in President Richard M. Nixon's announcement of his decision to resign as president rather than face impeachment hearings. The economy was also facing a recession; money and jobs were becoming scarcer.

Jackson's Operation PUSH was having problems, too. The organization was deeply in debt, and the government was investigating its financial records for suspected wrong-doing. The government and others were suspicious of Jackson's lifestyle among other things. In 1970 a private land trust had purchased a home for him in Chicago. Many believed the fifteen-room Romanesque home on Constance Avenue was a bit rich for the leader of poor people, and while Jackson and his family were hardly big spenders, over the years they had been the recipients of generous gifts from people who wished to help or were grateful for what Jackson had done.

In an interview with writer Barbara Reynolds, Jackson commented on the charges that he was living well at the expense of others:

> My value system is such that I don't have to live ostentatiously. They put the white leader in the White House. Why would anyone expect me to live in a mud hut? At least I deserve a Black House. There was a time when movement leaders were pushed so tight by the public that we couldn't get a house, we couldn't get a change of suit, we couldn't even go to the movies. . . . Well, I am committed to helping myself as well as others.

Jackson had labored long and hard to advance others as well as himself, and he believed it was reasonable that he reap some reward for all his efforts.

The government was unable to find anything wrong at Operation PUSH or with Jackson's personal finances, but the entire episode was unsettling for everyone involved, and while Jackson was victorious in this instance, another project of his was dying due to the economic recession. The Black Expo for that year had to be canceled because of lack of support. The economy had forced the closure of many black businesses, and those that survived were unwilling to risk investing in the event.

Bad luck seemed to follow bad luck. During the year, Jackson developed pneumonia. It was complicated by his sickle-cell anemia, and he was hospitalized for five days. Internally, PUSH was also facing problems. PUSH staff members began to complain about how the organization was being run. They believed they were not allowed enough responsibility; some resigned.

What was happening? Jackson wondered. Things seemed to be crumbling around him. As he always had in times of trouble, Jackson turned to prayer for answers. During a Baptist revival meeting in Kansas City, Missouri, that he had been asked to lead, Jackson fasted and prayed and, on Martin Luther King, Jr.'s birthday in 1974 he seemed to be given an answer.

That day Jackson was asked to lead a march in Washington, D.C., to commemorate Dr. King and to call attention to the jobless of the nation. The march was only a partial success. Many of the marchers appeared to be drunk or on drugs, a scene all too familiar in the inner city but surprising on a protest march. Looking about him, Jackson saw that there was a new problem in the United States, a problem he and PUSH might be able to help. There was a desperate need to combat drugs and poverty, but many adults were too far gone to be saved. Jackson came to the conclusion that the thing to do was to stop the tragedy of drugs before it devastated a human life, to appeal to the young people of the country. With young people, there was still a chance.

Out of Jackson's meditations and observations, the PUSH for Excellence (PUSH EXCEL) was born. "Our schools are infested with a steady diet of vandalism, violence, drugs, intercourse without discourse, alcohol and TV addiction," he stated. Something had to be done.

Starting in 1975, Jackson began traveling extensively around the country, speaking to teenagers, church congregations, teachers, and parents, urging them to save the lives of the young people. He spoke eloquently about his own childhood and illegitimacy. One problem blacks faced, he knew, was the high rate of teenage pregnancy. In his talks with teenagers, he was starkly frank with them, laying it on the line: "You're not a man because you can kill somebody. You're not a man because you can make a baby. They can make babies through artificial insemination. . . . You're a man only if you can raise a baby, protect a baby, and provide for a baby."

In his speeches Jackson urged parents to take an interest in their children, their schooling, their social lives, their television habits. In speaking to young people, he asked them to sign a pledge to spend two hours a night on

As head of PUSH EXCEL, Jackson traveled around the nation campaigning for jobs and economic equality for African Americans.

homework without distractions such as television and radio. Jackson also asked teachers to sign a pledge to take more interest in their students and to encourage them. Just as he had exhorted his Saturday listeners, he called upon his PUSH EXCEL listeners to be "somebody," asking them to adopt the slogan "Down with dope and up with hope!"

Because Jesse Jackson is an exciting and emotional speaker who can converse both in street language and in the speech of the establishment, his PUSH EXCEL message reached thousands and was taken to heart by thousands. Yet, as before, success brought its critics.

Some complained that the project was not complete; Jackson would speak and inspire teenagers, but PUSH provided no follow-up program for them. Despite criticism, however, PUSH EXCEL continued to succeed. Contributions began to flood in from both private and public sources, and by 1981 Operation PUSH was a huge organization, with the PUSH for Excellence project set up as a separate corporation and with Jackson on the go even more than before, flying about the country, exhorting and inspiring teenagers everywhere to make something of their lives.

During the 1970s, other things were happening in Jackson's life. He was now the father of five children: Santita, Jesse Jr., Jonathan Luther, Yusef DuBois, and Jacqueline II. The role of keeping the home together fell on Jacqueline's shoulders. Jesse was often gone, and if he was home, the house was filled with people wanting to talk with him, the phone ringing constantly. Jacqueline believed strongly in what Jesse was doing, however, and encouraged and supported him in all his efforts. Jackson was a loving father, devoting as much of his spare time as he could to his family. But by the late 1970s, Jackson's travels and plans were taking him farther afield.

Just as Jackson had always had a curiosity that, as a child, had spurred his desire to learn as much as possible in many different subjects, he also had a curiosity about the world and its different lands and cultures. During the civil rights movement his interest in Africa had deepened, as had that of many blacks. Many had a deep desire to know from where they, as a people, had come. In 1971 Jackson had been invited to go to Nigeria as part of an Afro-American cultural exchange, and he jumped at the opportunity. With Jacqueline and Santita by his side, he was finally able to visit the continent of his roots, to see what it was really like. The following year he visited Liberia, a country founded by freed American slaves.

As in all his endeavors, Jackson could not help becoming involved. In Liberia, Jackson tried unsuccessfully to gain dual citizenship for black Americans who owned land there, so they could live there without giving up their U.S.

citizenship. More successful was his 1973 campaign to raise money in the United States to help the drought-stricken nations of West Africa. Sixty-five tons of food and medical supplies were donated to help save lives.

Increasingly, too, Jackson was becoming aware of the problem of apartheid in the country of South Africa, an issue that would concern him throughout the 1980s. At the time, the system of apartheid in South Africa completely restricted where and how blacks could live and work. On a trip to South Africa in 1979, Jackson was, to his surprise, overwhelmingly welcomed by the black South Africans. He spoke to crowds of thousands, urging them to adopt the nonviolent methods of protest that had been so effective in the United States, and on his return to the United States, he spoke to businesses and governmental officials, pleading with them to withdraw their interests from South Africa until the yoke of apartheid was broken. He urged

Jesse Jackson and his wife, Jacqueline.

them to follow a list of principles that had been set forth in 1977 by the Reverend Leon Sullivan, the member of SCLC whose successful tactic of boycotting businesses in Philadelphia Jackson had followed when he headed Operation Breadbasket in Chicago. The Sullivan Principles included giving black South Africans jobs whenever possible and making efforts not to further the cause of apartheid.

In September of that same year, Jackson took a trip that was not so successful, one that would return to haunt him during his bids for the presidency. He traveled to Israel with the purpose of gaining Israeli acceptance and support of the Palestine Liberation Organization (PLO), which represented the refugees who had been forced from their lands when Israel was created in 1948. The Arab population of Israel, he believed, was downtrodden—many people had been displaced from their homes and homeland by the creation of the Israeli state—and, like the poor and homeless in America, deserved help.

Unlike South Africa, where he was at least tolerated by the white leaders, Jackson met outright hostility in Israel. Israeli leaders refused even to meet with him. He also alienated many Israeli and American Jews by comparing the Holocaust during World War II with what the blacks had suffered under slavery in the United States. Israelis and many Americans criticized him when he met with—and embraced—Yasir Arafat, the PLO leader. To his critics, it seemed that Jackson was endorsing the terrorist tactics the PLO employed in its fight for a homeland.

Jackson's trip to the Middle East marked his first formal attempts at international diplomacy. During a visit with Egyptian president Anwar el-Sadat, Sadat asked Jackson to take a message to Arafat asking for a cease-fire in order for negotiations to take place. Although Arafat refused Sadat's request, he remained friendly to Jackson, allowing him a hope for some future negotiations.

By 1980 the stage was set for Jackson to move on to

even bigger things. During the 1970s, he had had a taste of politics, had achieved national and international renown, and had shown that there was no problem he was afraid to tackle. Increasingly, his followers were asking themselves, "Why doesn't he run for president?" The time was fast approaching when Jackson would give them an answer.

10

"OUR TIME HAS COME!"

y 1979 Jesse Jackson's appearance was more conservative. The bushy Afro and the medallions had been replaced by a short haircut and a Brooks Brothers suit. Operation PUSH was a success, PUSH for Excellence was a success, and Jackson's dress and demeanor reflected this. Although his outward appearance had changed, he was still as deeply committed as ever to the causes he espoused, and he continued promoting them with the same energetic and flamboyant style.

In October of that year two of Jackson's coworkers with Operation PUSH, Frank Watkins and Bernard Lafayette, came to him with a new idea. They had been discussing it all evening, and barging in on Jackson as he relaxed at home in Chicago, they put it to him. Would he run for president? Initially, Jackson scoffed at the idea, but the thought had been planted in his mind, and over the next several years he began to consider the idea seriously. One incident in particular helped make up his mind.

Since the death of Mayor Richard J. Daley, Chicago politics had not changed much for African Americans. Daley's machine had, to a great extent, been eroded by his death, but blacks were still underrepresented in local government. In 1983, black congressman Harold Washington was running to unseat incumbent mayor Jane Byrne, who was also being challenged in the primary by Richard M. Daley, the son of Richard J. Daley. The black communities were solidly united behind Washington, but Washington believed he needed votes from the white communities to win the primary. To get those votes, he would need endorsements.

Jackson had enthusiastically supported Washington and now joined with him in an appeal for support. Washington asked Senator Edward M. Kennedy and former vice president Walter F. Mondale to endorse him. Both Mondale and Kennedy were liberals, and both had worked with Washington in Congress. To Jackson's dismay and anger, Mondale and Kennedy refused. They had old debts to pay, they said, despite the fact that they agreed Washington would be the best man for the job. Kennedy endorsed Jane Byrne, who in 1980 had supported his presidential bid against Jimmy Carter. Mondale endorsed Daley, who had supported the Carter-Mondale presidential ticket earlier.

Jackson was furious. So that's how politics works, he thought. Despite the fact that both Kennedy and Mondale had admitted they believed Washington to be the best candidate, they would not support him. Yet blacks were clamoring for a stronger voice in government. Despite the lack of endorsements by powerful white liberals, Harold Washington went on to win the Democratic mayoral primary in Chicago with overwhelming black support, garnering six out of every seven black votes. As Jackson exclaimed on television the night of the primary election, "Our time has come!"

The idea of "our time" and "It's our turn" were to become not only slogans for Harold Washington's race against Republican candidate Bernard Epton, whom Washington easily beat later in November, but rallying cries for Jackson's own presidential campaign. The seeds planted in 1979 had grown to fruition: Jackson would run for president; blacks *would* have a voice.

Jackson, however, still hesitated before formally announcing his decision. Did he really have the necessary support? During the summer of 1983, he began to test the waters. At the yearly conference of Operation PUSH members, Jackson brought up the subject in one of his speeches and was met with overwhelming enthusiasm. Cheering, clapping, and whistling, the fifteen hundred listeners rose to their feet shouting, "Run, Jesse, run!" Jackson met with this same reaction in August when he spoke to the crowds gathered at the Lincoln Memorial to celebrate the twentieth anniversary of the march on Washington. Again, the cries of "Run, Jesse, run!" filled the air.

Still, when Jackson broached the subject with black leaders and, in particular, the Coalition for 1984 Election Strategy, a group composed of fifty or so elected black officials, the reaction was mixed. Many did not want a black candidate at all; the time was not right. Others considered the idea but believed Jesse Jackson was not the man. He was too young, too much the showman, too unpredictable and impulsive.

But Jesse Jackson, after years of working with the ordinary people—the voters—believed he knew what they wanted and how to appeal to them. On November 2, 1983, Jackson flew to Washington, D.C., to witness the signing by President Ronald Reagan of a bill establishing Martin Luther King, Jr.'s birthday as a national holiday. On the next day, November 3, at a rally of twenty-five hundred supporters at the Washington Convention

Center, Jackson announced his formal intention to run for president. He said:

> I embark upon this course with a sense of inner confidence. I offer myself to the American people, not as a perfect servant, but as a public servant. I offer myself and my service as a vehicle to give a voice to the voiceless, representation to the unrepresented and hope to the downtrodden. . . .
>
> Let the word go forth from this occasion that this candidacy is not for blacks only. . . . I would like to use this candidacy to help build a new rainbow coalition of the rejected that will include whites, blacks, Hispanics, Indians, and Native Americans, Asians, women, young people, poor people, old people, gay people, laborers, small farmers, small business-persons, peace activists and environmentalists. . . . Together, the old minorities constitute a new majority. Together we can build a new majority. . . .

The idea of a "rainbow coalition" had originated, of course, with his Operation PUSH. Now Jackson formalized it on a national level, naming his political party the Rainbow Coalition. He wanted to involve all who had been left out of the political process, to give them a voice, through their candidate, in their own lives and in their government.

Jackson had picked a hard row to hoe. He was entering the presidential race late—there were already seven Democratic candidates facing Ronald Reagan—and he had no organization, almost no campaign funds, no campaign plans, no manager. Many black leaders resented his candidacy, believing he was running merely to gratify his own ego and resenting the fact that he continued to pursue the presidency despite the objections they had raised. Other black leaders saw Jackson's emphasis on being a "black" candidate as divisive rather than unifying. Instead of bringing people together racially, they believed his candidacy was setting blacks apart yet again. It was also divisive because it drew votes away from Walter Mondale, the Democratic front-runner, and in a race with the votes split between Jackson and Mondale, Ronald Reagan could come out the winner.

Despite the rumblings of dissatisfaction, Jackson forged ahead with his campaign, hiring Arnold Pinkney as his campaign manager. Pinkney had twice helped Carl Stokes campaign successfully to be mayor of Cleveland. Despite limited funds, he and Jackson immediately began a campaign for the New Hampshire primary, the first primary race to be held. Then, early in December 1983, an opportunity to gain goodwill and publicity was handed to Jackson: During a raid on Syrian antiaircraft guns in Lebanon, an American plane had been shot down and its pilot taken hostage. Lieutenant Robert O. Goodman, Jr., was both black and from New Hampshire. What better way to ingratiate oneself to New Hampshire and to America than to obtain the release of Goodman? Jackson immediately began looking into the idea.

On the strength of the ties he had established in the Middle East during his 1979 trip, Jackson flew to Syria and began negotiating. President Reagan had tried to discourage Jackson from making the journey, saying that "sometimes efforts of this kind can be counterproductive . . . and it's possible that sometimes someone with the best of intentions could change the balance unfavorably."

In Damascus, Jackson was granted an interview with Syria's president, Hafez al-Assad. During the interview, Jackson pleaded with Assad to release Goodman. Assad was not encouraging but said he would consider it. The next day, Jackson was elated when Syria's foreign minister announced that Assad would permit the release of Goodman.

Jackson's return home with Robert Goodman at his side warranted a hero's welcome. President Reagan, all his doubts seemingly forgotten, invited Jackson to the White House and lauded his efforts. Suddenly, in the eyes of many Americans who had been hesitant about him before, Jackson was a viable political candidate. After all, he could

Jackson and Lieutenant Robert Goodman, Jr., arrive at Andrews Air Force Base in Maryland.

deal diplomatically in the Middle East, that unpredictable area of the world where so many had failed before.

Eight days before the New Hampshire primary, however, Jackson made a devastating mistake. Jewish voters had not forgotten Jackson's sympathy with the PLO in 1979, and it still rankled them. In February 1984, Milton Coleman, a black reporter for *The Washington Post*, reported that Jackson had made a negative comment about Jewish people in a private conversation, denigrating Jewish people and New York City. The press and the public pounced on the information with malicious glee while Jackson pondered what to do about what had been a careless joke. He traveled to a Jewish synagogue in Manchester, New Hampshire, to make a public apology, saying, "It was not in the spirit of meanness but an off-color remark having no bearing on religion and politics." Many, however, believed the apology was too little, too late, and inappropriate for a man seeking the presidency. The whole incident tarnished Jackson's campaign, and he finished fourth in the New Hampshire primary with 5 percent of the vote, tying former senator George McGovern and, oddly, President Ronald Reagan, for whom many Democrats had voted as a write-in candidate.

After his defeat in New Hampshire, Jackson threw himself even more into the campaign, working for victories on "Super Tuesday," the day five states hold their primaries. Again, however, the charge of anti-Semitism reared its head. On March 11, 1984, in a series of statements, Louis Farrakhan, a well-known Black Muslim leader and a supporter of Jackson for president, appeared to threaten the life of reporter Milton Coleman, who had earlier reported Jackson's comment. Farrakhan also made a number of comments that were construed as anti-Semitic. In one, he called Hitler a great man. Because Farrakhan was a Jackson supporter and because his "Fruits of Islam" had provided bodyguards for Jackson before Jackson was assigned Secret Service agents, many took Farrakhan's sentiments to be Jackson's, also. If any Jewish voters had been wavering, they were now firmly against Jackson.

Despite the damage, Jackson waged a good campaign, coupling it with voter registration drives. Although many black leaders abandoned him, he found that black voters flocked to him and to the Rainbow Coalition. On Super Tuesday, Jackson surprised everyone by winning major blocks of voters in three southern states. Later, on May 1, he won his first primary in the District of Columbia.

When the campaign dust cleared, Jackson had won 384 delegates to the Democratic National Convention. Although this was not enough to give him the Democratic nomination, it did give Jackson the power to influence the Democratic Party platform and gained him a new respect among old-line Democrats. On July 17, 1984, he was invited to address the convention. As he ended his speech, he reminded his listeners:

> Our flag is red, white and blue, but our nation is a rainbow—red, yellow, brown, black and white—we're all precious in God's sight. America is not like a blanket— one piece of unbroken cloth, the same color, the same texture, the same size. America is more like a quilt—many patches, many pieces, many colors, many sizes, all woven and held together by a common thread.

In many ways, Jesse Jackson's campaign for president was a success. By the end of the 1984 campaign, Jackson was no longer just a civil rights leader. He was a leader of people. Despite the problems he had encountered during his campaign, he had proved himself to be a viable

Jackson's ability to get votes in presidential primaries made him a force to be reckoned with by the nation's black leaders. He is shown here in Washington, D.C., with, from left, Dorothy Height, head of the National Council of Negro Women; Richard Hatcher, former mayor of Gary, Indiana; Ronald H. Brown, head of the Democratic National Committee; and Charles Rangel, Democratic congressman from New York City.

candidate able to stir both the hearts and minds of his followers. He had also shown himself to be adept at foreign diplomacy, a necessary quality in a president.

Jackson's defeat came not because he was unqualified but because he was battling a number of factors: his own inexperience, a lack of support from established black leaders, and the fact that he was the only black candidate to make a strenuous and serious bid for the presidency. The times also were against him. The 1970s had ended with a disillusionment with government and governmental officials—and with causes. The decade of the eighties was well under way, a time in which those with the greatest political influence (the middle, upper-middle, and upper classes) were turning away from social issues and focusing on making more and more money and acquiring more and more possessions, often at the expense of the lower classes. Jackson's time had not yet come.

11

"WIN, JESSE, WIN!"

nlike many who have run for political office and lost, Jesse Jackson was not one to disappear into obscurity only to be mentioned in a "Where Are They Now?" column. After the 1984 campaign, Jackson once again took up the reins of Operation PUSH in Chicago and returned to his Saturday morning preaching. His life was back to normal—or as normal as it can be if one is Jesse Jackson. Of his children, in 1984 only Yusef and his youngest daughter, Jacqueline II, were at home; the others were at college. Santita was a premedical student at Howard University in Washington, D.C.; Jesse Jr., and Jonathan were attending Jackson's alma mater, A&T (now North Carolina Agricultural and Technical State University), in Greensboro. The big house in Chicago was not silent, however, for Jackson was constantly holding meetings in its rooms, the phone ringing in the background.

Although he had lost the presidential nomination, Jackson now saw himself as the conscience of the nation and continued to develop his Rainbow Coalition, flying between Chicago and Washington, D.C. He believed the country needed to be reminded of its problems and the problems of the world. In January 1985, in response to President Reagan's inauguration ceremonies, he led a "counterinaugural" march in Washington. In March he led a re-creation of the Selma march with other black leaders. When Reagan met with the Soviet leader, Mikhail Gorbachev, in Geneva, Switzerland, Jackson flew to Geneva and independently met with Gorbachev to discuss discrimination in the Soviet Union against Soviet Jews. Jackson pleaded on their behalf, asking that the Soviet Union allow their emigration to Israel or the United States. He also continued his demonstrations against apartheid in South Africa, leading marches in Washington and challenging U.S. businesses to adhere to the Sullivan Principles or withdraw their interests from South Africa. When Jackson was not nudging America's conscience, he was visiting other countries, establishing valuable ties with various foreign leaders. One was never sure where he would pop up next.

In 1986, Jackson announced a new National Rainbow Coalition that would be a "progressive force" in the Democratic Party. It was not until 1987, however, that he declared himself a presidential candidate yet again, seeking the 1988 Democratic nomination. His 1984 supporters were jubilant, but others were puzzled. He had been defeated once, why try again? His critics could not see that Jackson, although he intended to run a race to win, also had other objectives. The most important objective was that of giving minorities—the "voiceless"—a voice, and he saw himself as that voice.

Much had changed since his 1984 campaign, both politically and personally for Jesse Jackson. The intervening years had been good to Jackson. When, as is required of all presidential candidates, he released his personal income statements, they revealed that he and his wife, Jacqueline, were now among the well-to-do. In 1984, his total income had been reported at $59,453; by 1987, the Jacksons' combined incomes were reported at $209,358. Much of their income—$192,090—had come from Personalities International, Inc., a corporation founded to provide management for celebrities and headed by Jacqueline Jackson. Although the corporation had a number of clients, most of its business was handling Jackson's earnings from his speeches and publications. In addition to income, the Jacksons also reported a number of assets. The largest asset was shares with value of more than $250,000 in the Inner City Broadcasting Company, a company that owned several radio stations, the Apollo Theater in New York City, and some cable television interests. In total, Jackson's income and assets were around the million-dollar mark. Jackson had come a long way from earning nickels in a woodyard as a child.

Politically, too, things appeared more favorable for Jackson. Whereas in 1984 Walter Mondale was clearly the Democratic front-runner, in 1988 the Democratic Party had no obvious contenders. During 1987 it seemed that nearly every Democrat of any renown was declaring himself a candidate. The field of choices was large, and the public tended to confuse the candidates: They all seemed so similar—except for Jesse Jackson. Suddenly his color and reputation were advantages. Everyone knew who Jackson was, and amid the crowd of white Democrats, he stood out.

In 1984, a majority of black leaders in the country had refrained from giving Jackson their support. Now they were eager to support him. He had proved that he could get the votes and was popular among many voters. He was now trying to reach all voters, although he still appealed to the poor and blacks. And he offered answers to some of America's most serious problems. Where the other candidates hedged on solutions to the budget deficit, for example, Jackson exhorted his listeners to support him in increasing the taxes of the wealthy and in cutting defense spending. This was what small farmers and others caught in a credit crunch wanted to hear.

Going into the Democratic primaries, Jackson was clearly a front-runner because of his public renown. The first two primaries were to be held in Iowa and New Hampshire in March of 1988. Jackson decided to focus on Iowa because it was a less conservative state than New Hampshire and he stood a better chance of winning. Even so, he could not wage the kind of campaign the other candidates could, because of low funds—$45,000 was allotted for the campaign in Iowa, whereas the other candidates spent nearly a million dollars each. Although Jackson did not win in Iowa, he garnered 11 percent of the votes, a respectable number. In New Hampshire that day, he received 8 percent of the vote.

Later primaries proved Jackson's strength as a candidate. In Minnesota, Maine, and Vermont, he came in second, and on Super Tuesday, he surprised a large number of people by winning five states outright.

Throughout the 1980s, candidates for public office had become increasingly aware of the importance of the black vote. By 1988, blacks made up 11 percent of the voting-age population, and more and more of them were registering to vote. In an article entitled "Poll Power," *Life* magazine reported that "blacks, ages 18 to 24, whose [voter] registration rates caught up to whites of the same age in 1984, passed whites in 1986: 46 percent of young blacks versus 42 percent of young whites were registered." The number of black voters was increasing, and Jackson's victories in various primaries served only to reinforce the need for any candidate to go after the black vote. Suddenly other candidates began to speak of some of the same things as Jackson. Richard Gephardt and Michael Dukakis, for example, started mentioning the idea of funding the African National Congress, a major anti-apartheid group in South Africa, an organization Jackson had supported for years. Jackson was certainly having an influence on the campaign, and although most analysts doubted he could win the presidential nomination, there was increasing talk of Jackson as vice president.

Jackson's biggest victory came in April 1988 in the Michigan primary. By that time the race had narrowed to one between Massachusetts governor Michael Dukakis and Jackson. Dukakis had spent nearly a million dollars campaigning in Michigan and had the endorsement of a number of local politicians, including Coleman Young, Detroit's black mayor. Everyone expected Dukakis to win easily. But they had not counted on Jesse Jackson. Jackson had gone out onto the streets of Michigan cities to shake hands and speak to people, appealing to everyone. Unlike Dukakis, Jackson could not afford expensive TV coverage, so he went directly to the voters. And it paid off. When the results were in, Jackson had won the Michigan primary with a whopping 54 percent of the vote, the biggest win of any of the Democratic candidates outside their home states.

Suddenly Jackson was hot. Campaign contributions began to roll in. Instead of chanting "Run, Jesse, run," his audiences began yelling "Win, Jesse, win!" Jackson himself said, in an April issue of *Time*, that it "may take just one more major Jackson victory for the Democrats to seriously revise their calculation about whether a black preacher-politician who has never held public office can actually win the presidential nomination."

Jackson's platform—the things he was advocating be done if he were president—was an outgrowth of all he had done over the years. As he always had, since his visit to South Africa in the 1970s, he called for the withdrawal of U.S. companies until South Africa dismantled its system of apartheid. Among other issues, he also proposed a freeze

on defense spending and on tax hikes, along with the
elimination of many of the tax deductions that benefited
middle- and upper-class taxpayers. He supported the
ideas of an intensive war on drugs, government financing
of low-income housing, and a federally run health insur-
ance program. All of these were things for which he had
worked as head of Operation PUSH.

There was a change in one of Jackson's positions,
however. While still supporting the right of the Palestinian
people to an independent homeland and government, he
announced that he also supported the right of Israel to
exist within secure boundaries, and in 1988, he rejected a
meeting with PLO leader Yasir Arafat. Jackson was keenly
aware of the damage done by his offhand remark in 1984
about Jewish people. In 1988, he was trying to mend
fences. Unfortunately, at least in New York City, it did not
work.

As the April 19 New York primary drew closer, the New
York City papers began recalling Jackson's 1984 remarks;
the city had still not forgiven him. New York's feisty mayor,
Edward Koch, spoke out against Jackson, saying, "Jews
and other supporters of Israel have got to be crazy to vote
for Jesse Jackson." Rumors circulated that Jackson had
kept up a secret friendship with Black Muslim leader Louis
Farrakhan, even after he had denounced Farrakhan in
1984 for his anti-Semitic remarks.

Jackson chose to ignore Koch's and others' rehashing
of 1984, gaining instead the support of David Dinkins,
who was later elected mayor of New York City. Jackson
spoke out against drugs and avoided the Jewish issue alto-
gether. Unfortunately, Koch had the louder voice, and
when the returns were in, Michael Dukakis had won with
51 percent of the vote. Jackson came in second with 37
percent. If Jackson had been able to win New York, it
would have given him the delegate strength to mount a
serious challenge to Dukakis for—and perhaps to win—

the presidential nomination at the Democratic National Convention.

With the major primaries over, Jackson saw his job as winning as many more delegates as he could to enable him to influence the Democratic platform and perhaps gain the vice-presidential nomination at the national convention in August 1988.

Although he had all but lost the presidential nomination, Jackson was still perceived as a threat by some. On May 18, 1988, a Missouri couple, Londell and Tammy Williams, were arrested on the charge of plotting to kill Jackson, either on June 21 or July 4. Jackson, who was campaigning in California at the time, praised the efforts of the law enforcement officers who had discovered the plot, but he shrugged off the incident. As he later said, "I know every day I face real threats. But I must be willing to take the risk and pay the price. . . . A dreamer can be stopped, but the dream will not stop."

As the Democratic National Convention approached, Jackson's hopes for the vice-presidential nomination grew stronger. He and Jacqueline were invited to spend the Fourth of July with front-runner Michael Dukakis and his wife, Kitty. Everything seemed to be going Jackson's way. Then, on July 12, the rug was snatched from beneath him.

Just days before the Democratic National Convention was to open, Michael Dukakis finally announced his choice of a running mate: Texas senator Lloyd Bentsen. The announcement was handled poorly by Dukakis in that he had not telephoned Jackson and told him of the decision in advance. Jackson learned he had lost the vice-presidential nomination in an airport from a reporter. Cut to the quick, Jackson refused any comment at that time. After several hours of thinking, Jackson called a press conference. Although icy in demeanor, Jackson said, "I'm too mature to be angry. I'm focused on what we must do to keep hope alive." But he refused to say at that time whether or not he would support the Democratic ticket.

Although Jackson had said he was more hurt than angry, many of his followers were furious at the slight. They demanded to know how blacks could continue to serve the Democratic Party when it was clear that their color prevented them from being on the national ticket. They regretted having been obedient and loyal Democrats and allowing their political strength to be fragmented.

Dukakis called Jackson with an apology after the announcement was made, but the damage was done. As both men headed for the convention, they were aware that a deal would have to be made if Dukakis were to gain Jackson's support and that of his followers. On Monday, just hours before the convention was to begin, Jesse Jackson and Michael Dukakis and their campaign managers sat down to negotiate. After three hours, they came to an agreement: Jackson would play a significant part in Dukakis's campaign and would give a speech at the convention introducing Dukakis. Jackson, however, was unable to get any of his proposals adopted as part of the Democratic platform; if Dukakis were elected, there would be none of the stirring social changes Jackson had envisioned.

The second night of the convention was an emotional and tense one. It was the night Jackson was to speak, and people wondered if he would show any bitterness over the treatment he had received. When asked who he wanted to introduce him, Jackson replied, "The Jackson Five," referring to his children, who had campaigned tirelessly for him.

That night all five of Jackson's children filed onto the platform and spoke with praise and love of their father. Jesse Jr. ended their introduction, saying, "We the children of Jesse and Jacqueline Jackson are proud to be Jacksons." The crowd leapt to its feet, cheering the group of intelligent and attractive youngsters.

Jackson's moving speech, delivered in his flamboyant, preacher style, roused the audience. In it, he recounted his long journey over time to reach his position at the convention, and he thanked all who had helped him. Then, he threw his support behind the Dukakis-Bentsen ticket, urged his supporters to do the same, and turned the stage over to Dukakis, who was quickly nominated and confirmed as the Democratic presidential nominee. The next month the Republicans nominated George Bush and Dan Quayle to run against Dukakis and Bentsen.

Part of the agreement with Dukakis was that Jackson would be given a plane and would travel, speak, and raise funds for the Dukakis-Bentsen ticket during the fall campaign. These conditions were a step up for Jackson. As *The New York Times* reported, "Gone are the days of the Presidential primary when Mr. Jackson's chartered DC-9 was a virtual legend, a crumbling campaign plane without such luxuries as a stove. . . . Now, Mr. Jackson's chartered plane is carpeted. It has a television and a videocassette player. Delicacies are served. . . ."

Jackson, however, did not have much time for luxuries. True to his promise, he threw himself into the campaign, tirelessly traveling and speaking throughout the country. He wanted to see Dukakis elected, not only to oust the Republicans from the White House, but also because, if Dukakis were elected, Jackson knew he would be rewarded for his efforts in some way. He would then be able to try to effect some of the changes he envisioned for America. But this was not to be.

In November 1988 George Bush won an overwhelming victory for the Republican Party, with 426 electoral votes to Dukakis's 112. Because of Jackson's efforts and popularity, however, one place Dukakis did win was the District of Columbia. Jackson was to remember this and see it later as an opportunity for himself.

The 1988 election was, for Jackson, both a loss and a victory. Although he had failed in his efforts to obtain one of the top two spots on the Democratic ticket, he won in terms of personal satisfaction, influence, and recognition. Never before in America had a black candidate come that close to winning a major party nomination for president, and Jackson was just beginning to reap the rewards for that achievement.

12

ONWARD

More than in 1984, Jesse Jackson's 1988 bid for the presidency stirred and changed attitudes among voters, particularly among white voters. Although some still resisted the idea of a black candidate, more and more were accepting the idea that it was okay—a black man could make a good president. During the fall of 1988, while campaigning for Dukakis, Jackson reinforced this idea in the minds of his listeners through his electric personality and his speeches. It certainly helped Dukakis, and did not hurt Jackson, who perhaps was already beginning to build a support base for a run in 1992.

Some of the tactics Jackson used, however, did not quite work. In 1984, he had been able to negotiate the release of Lieutenant Robert Goodman and had assumed the mantle of hero in the eyes of many in the United States. In 1988, he attempted a similar move, only to be frustrated in his efforts.

At that time terrorist groups with ties to Iran were holding a number of Americans hostage. Toward the end of July, Jackson offered his help in trying to persuade Iran's foreign minister, Ali Akbar Velayati, to assist in obtaining the hostages' freedom.

Jackson's intentions were threefold. Success in negotiating the hostages' release would bring glory to himself. It would also benefit Michael Dukakis, whom he was supporting. Finally, it would affirm Jackson as an able foreign policy negotiator in the eyes of both Dukakis and the public, and make him a contender for the office of secretary of state under Dukakis, if Dukakis were to win the presidency.

Jackson had expected the Reagan administration to try to dissuade him from traveling to Iran. He had not expected that Michael Dukakis would also be cool to the idea. Rather than firmly supporting Jackson's efforts, Dukakis initially made a vague statement to the effect that such efforts should be left to the government and that private citizens should not get involved in such matters. Stung by Dukakis's lack of support, Jackson backed off and left the hostage issue alone for the time being.

In the November presidential election, former vice president George Bush won handily. While the Republican win was a blow to Jesse Jackson, he did not mourn his loss for long. He resumed his usual frenetic schedule. He oversaw the activities of Operation PUSH, although he was no longer its president, having resigned his position when he declared his candidacy for the Democratic presidential nomination. He started preaching again. He also spoke out on the issue of terminology for black Americans.

Some blacks believed the term *African American* most clearly expressed both pride in their African heritage and determination to be treated as full citizens of the United States. But the new term was not well known until Jesse Jackson spoke out in its favor and began to use it himself. Once Jackson took up the cause, more and more people, black and white, began to favor the term over *black* or *Afro-American*. So did more and more print and broadcast media.

By 1989 Jackson was spending less and less time in Chicago and more and more in Washington, D.C., with his Rainbow Coalition. He and Jacqueline had bought a home in Washington.

Back in Chicago, Jackson's candidate of choice in the early 1980s, Harold Washington, had won a second term in 1987 but, tragically, had died after serving only seven months. A special election was called, and Richard M. Daley was the front-running Democratic candidate. He was seriously challenged by Tim Evans, a black politician running on a third-party ticket. Everyone in the black community expected Jackson to support Evans against Daley, Jackson's longtime political foe, and he did not fail them. However, the state Democrats, believing they had done a great deal for Jackson's bid for president, expected him to support Daley. When he announced he would support Evans, Jackson angered many in the party.

In March 1989, in a letter to an Illinois congressman, Jackson appeared to suggest that he would drop his support of Evans if the state's Democratic Party pledged to support him in a 1992 presidential bid. When confronted with it by the press, Jackson said the letter was merely intended to show how support can be somewhat hypocritical, as in 1983 when Harold Washington was unable to get the endorsements of Mondale and Kennedy. He was one hundred percent behind Evans, he said. Yet the whole episode left a shadow over the campaign that had already renewed some of the hostilities between blacks and whites in Chicago. In the mayoral race, Daley beat Evans resoundingly, and Jackson turned his attention to his "new" city of Washington, D.C.

Jackson had not forgotten the poor, the homeless, the ones who looked to him for a voice. He was on the road speaking for them again, and his voice now sounded throughout the world as well as the United States. In January 1989 Jackson flew to Moscow to try to gather aid for Armenian earthquake victims and again to discuss Soviet human rights. On returning to the United States, he also spoke out about crime in the cities. In April, he appeared in a guest spot on the NBC-TV sitcom *A Different World*, in which he convinced the show's characters that they should "stand up for what you believe in."

That same month, Jackson let it be known that he was considering running for mayor of Washington, D.C. If he chose to do so, he would be almost assured of a victory. The incumbent, Marion S. Barry, had been arrested for drug use, and the city government was in disarray. Jackson had always spoken out vehemently against drugs, and it was thought that no such scandal would ever occur with him. The population of Washington, D.C., was predominantly African American, and just as blacks had seen

When Mayor Marion Barry was convicted of using drugs and resigned his office, Jackson considered running for mayor of the nation's capital.

Jackson as their hope in the presidential primary, they would most likely back him if he chose to run for mayor.

The position of mayor carried with it several benefits for Jackson. He would be an influential political figure in the midst of the heart of politics, the nation's capital. The office would also have allowed Jackson to tackle some of the problems he had traditionally fought. Washington had a very high crime rate, a severe drug problem, and a rising high school dropout rate. Jackson had fought these before, and he could greatly benefit the ailing city with his experience, ideas, and programs. Finally, the office of mayor was an elective one. One major criticism against Jackson in both his 1984 and 1988 campaigns had been that he had never held elected office. If he ran for mayor of Washington and won, as he undoubtedly would, this would silence that criticism. But Washington, D.C., had so many problems. If he were elected and did not solve the problems, he feared that any hopes he harbored for the 1992 presidential race would evaporate. Throughout 1989 Jackson wavered in his decision. But he and his family officially moved to the district in the fall so he could legally run for mayor if he chose to.

In January 1990 Jackson decided that the office of mayor was not for him. There were alternatives, however. Throughout the 1988 campaign, Jackson had often spoken for the idea of statehood for the District of Columbia, garnering a great deal of enthusiastic support for it from Washington voters. The district has a bigger population than some states, yet it has no voting representation in Congress. Jackson would devote his time to this issue, he decided, and to improving the moral tenor of the city, rather than run for mayor. But before he could turn to that effort, Jackson had something else he wished to do.

Jackson had spoken out loudly against apartheid in South Africa since the 1970s. In January 1990 the government of South Africa announced that it would recognize the African National Congress and would soon release

Nelson Mandela, the South African anti-apartheid leader who had been imprisoned since 1962. Mandela had become a symbol of the anti-apartheid movement. As a civil rights leader in the United States and a supporter of Mandela, Jackson wanted at least to meet and speak with him.

On February 7, 1990, Jackson arrived in South Africa, despite discouragement from its government, which pleaded concern for Jackson's safety, fearing he might be threatened by dissident whites. But among South African blacks, his visit was seen as the most important by an American since Robert F. Kennedy's in 1966. After numerous speeches, Jackson finally met with Nelson Mandela in prison. He cemented a friendship with the leader that would later prove useful when Mandela visited the United States and essentially gave his blessing to Jackson's campaign for "shadow senator" of Washington, D.C. The office of "shadow senator" was created to push for statehood for the district.

Jackson had decided to run for shadow senator after turning away from the idea of campaigning for mayor. As shadow senator, he would be an unpaid lobbyist for statehood. Even though it is not an official federal position, Jackson would at last be an elected official, putting to rest the criticism that he had never held elected office. In February, when he broached the subject of running for shadow senator at a National Governors' Association dinner in Washington, one Democrat said, "That son of a gun is running for president again." Jackson waged his campaign for shadow senator with the same skill, flair for the dramatic, and tactics he had used so well when running for president.

In August 1990, when Iraq's president, Saddam Hussein, ordered the invasion of Kuwait, Jackson spoke against it and set to work to involve himself in some way to help. At the same time the Kuwaiti situation was evolving, Jackson was putting together the idea for a television talk

Jackson and his family moved to Washington, D.C., because Jackson wanted to help fight for statehood for the District. He is shown here at a rally for statehood.

show. The show was intended to air opinions on such issues as the plight of the poor and the future of the small farmer. It would not be, according to Jackson, "just reflecting and recording and research. We intend to communicate, to act, to make things happen." Jackson's television contacts at this time were to prove useful. Saddam Hussein was holding thousands of foreigners who had been in Kuwait as "guests" of Iraq, refusing to release them. It was a situation made-to-order for Jackson.

The only foreigners being allowed to travel freely into and out of Iraq were journalists. Because Jackson's own television show would not premiere until the first weekend of October 1990, he could not travel to Iraq on behalf of his own show. Using his connections, however, Jackson was able to go to Iraq the first week of September on behalf of *Inside Edition*, a syndicated television show.

Once in Iraq, Jackson met with Saddam Hussein for a short interview and begged the president to release the hostages. A few hours later, the announcement came that a group of hostages would be released. Whether Jackson influenced that decision, however, is widely debated. During their interview, Saddam had appeared unmoved by Jackson's eloquence, and some analysts speculate that it was the situation more than Jackson's action that influenced Saddam. Saddam Hussein, at the time, was trying to project an image of being tough but willing to talk. If he had not agreed to Jackson's plea, many believe, it would have seemed as if he were unwilling to listen or talk at all. Whatever the answer is, the result was beneficial to Jackson politically. Several days later, he disembarked in New York in triumph from a plane carrying a group of newly freed hostages.

As the new year 1991 was ushered in, Jackson seemed well on his way to another bid for the presidency. He had once again proved himself an able negotiator in foreign affairs. He was in the public eye each week on his television show, and on January 2, 1991, he was sworn in as shadow senator of the District of Columbia.

All this public exposure spelled success and potential to many, yet there were problems. Many of Jackson's critics said he had little or nothing to do with Saddam Hussein's decision to release the hostage group. His television show, rather than capturing his flamboyant and electric style, was criticized as being dry and dull, with sets that resembled a faculty lounge in a poor high school. Critics also pointed out that the office of shadow senator was just that—without substance—and said it did not help Jesse Jackson's chances in 1992.

Jackson objected to the term "shadow" senator. "It's United States Senator from Washington," he would protest. In fact, the word *shadow* was not on the ballot when he was voted into the office in November 1990. However, in reality he was not United States senator from Washington, but an unpaid lobbyist to the Senate from the District of Columbia. He did not have any real power; nor did he enjoy any of the privileges of the Senate, such as access to the Senate floor or an office. This lack of power rankled him, considering, as he would sometimes point out, that he had gotten more votes than many senators from sparsely populated states. All he could do was work behind the scenes—an unfamiliar place for Jesse Jackson—to advance the goal of winning statehood for the district. If that goal were reached, then there could be a real senator from the district—one with real power—and the people of the district would have real representation in the government. The question was: Should he continue to strive for that goal while also waging a campaign for the presidency in 1992? It was a decision he would have to make soon.

While he was making up his mind, several Democrats declared their candidacy for their party's presidential nomination in 1992, among them L. Douglas Wilder of Virginia, the first black governor of a southern state since the Reconstruction period after the Civil War. Although Jackson later stated that Wilder's candidacy had no influence on his decision, there is no question that if both he and Wilder ran, the black vote would have been split between the two black candidates.

Other concerns included the fear that if he ran and lost a third time, he would never be taken seriously again. There was a general feeling that President Bush, running for a second term in office, would be hard to beat and that the chances for a Democratic victory would be much greater in 1996. Finally, Jackson had been offered the position as host of a weekly talk show for Cable News Network, provided he did not run in 1992.

On November 2, 1991, at a Washington, D.C., public housing project with a reputation for drugs and violence, Jesse Jackson, joined by his wife, Jackie, announced that he would not seek the Democratic presidential nomination. He also asked his backers not to support other candidates. "We are free agents in a political market," he told them, criticizing both the Republicans and the Democrats for "those caught in the middle." He called for a "new democratic majority" but did not call for the formation of a third political party. He did not go into detail about what he wanted his supporters to do, but observers speculated that he intended to use his supporters as leverage with other candidates to force them to take seriously the Rainbow Coalition agenda. This included national health care, affordable housing, and equal financing of education.

It also included statehood for the District of Columbia, the issue for which he had pledged to work as shadow senator. Of all the goals on the Rainbow Coalition agenda, this was the easiest to bring about. And if Jackson managed to win statehood, he would enjoy considerable political clout.

Many people were disappointed that Jackson would not be running for president in 1992. Some feared that he might lose his political interest if he stayed out of the race. But Jackson intended to lose nothing. He was "somebody" and he intended to stay that way. And in reality there was little chance that he would be forgotten, for he had made an indelible mark on American life in the latter part of the twentieth century.

His position as "somebody" was underscored by the U.S. Postal Service in February 1991 when it created a series of pictorial cancellations in honor of Black History Month. The cancellation mark included the likenesses of Dr. Martin Luther King, Jr., Sojourner Truth, Harriet Tubman, and Jesse Jackson. Not only was Jackson the only one of the four who was alive, he was only the second living American to be so honored. The first had been John Glenn, the astronaut who later served as senator from Ohio.

13

AND STILL
SEARCHING

overnor Bill Clinton of Arkansas won the Democratic presidential bid in the summer of 1992. The following November, he was elected president, besting Republican president George Bush. Many of the items on Clinton's agenda were ones that Jackson supported, such as national health care and improved race relations. Although Clinton's success in these areas would depend on his ability to persuade Congress—and the nation—to share his vision, he seemed a strong chief executive. Jesse Jackson realized that unless something unexpected happened, Clinton would win election to a second term. Jackson would not get the opportunity to run for president again anytime soon.

Still, Jackson kept himself in the limelight, seeking another outlet for his ambition. Marshall Frady, author of *Jesse: The Life and Pilgrimage of Jesse Jackson*, discussed Jackson on *Frontline* on public television in the spring of 1996: "If there was a riot in Los Angeles, he was there; a plant closing in Wisconsin, he was there; an earthquake in Armenia, he was there. . . . still searching for the big stage. . . . but the more he sought recognition, the more allergic the press grew toward him. The more he chased the moment, the more it seemed to flee his grasp."

Jackson realized that without official political standing, he was not going to achieve the recognition he wanted. He was comfortable staying in the public eye, voicing his opinions about a spectrum of issues, and he had proved his ability on his own television show. In fact, he was so good at hosting a news and public affairs program that in 1992, CNN offered him a new show, *Both Sides with Jesse Jackson.* This Sunday afternoon show was hailed by critics, who stated that Jackson presided with "calm assurance and legitimate curiosity" and gave "voice to the voiceless in a medium known for its narrow range of opinion in news and public affairs." The show provided Jackson with a forum to discuss a variety of current issues. But Jackson needed a cause, and a base. Three years later, he believed he had found it.

For Jesse Jackson, 1995 was a watershed year—a turning point. It was the year when former football star O. J. Simpson was tried in Los Angeles, California, for the murder of his wife, Nicole Brown Simpson, and her friend Ronald Goldman. The trial, Simpson's acquittal, and public reaction to these events revealed the deep racial fault lines that still existed in America. Most whites believed Simpson guilty. Many blacks—including those who made up the majority of the jury at Simpson's trial—charged that evidence against him had been planted by racist white Los Angeles police. This was also the year that Newt Gingrich, Republican congressman from Georgia, was elevated to the powerful position of Speaker of the House of Representatives. Gingrich led his fellow Republicans in a campaign for change. The Republican plan, called the "Contract with America," included passing a balanced budget and reducing the federal debt by cutting or reducing social-assistance programs. Many blacks and their white supporters believed that the Contract with America would destroy the gains that African Americans had made since the civil rights movement. Gingrich and his forces won additional seats in Congress in the 1994 elections. With even more Republicans in Congress, the Republican plan would have stronger support, and the Democratic president would have difficulty pushing through his own agenda.

For Jackson, the widening racial and economic gaps in the country demanded moral leadership. He was prepared to take up that responsibility. It was time for a new movement, time to march again. He immediately began to plan a three-day, thirty-mile march from Gingrich's Georgia district to the site of Martin Luther King, Jr.'s grave. Jackson hoped that thousands would participate, but only a few hundred people showed up. Many observers said Jackson's politics were a thing of the past, that his time was over.

Far more in the spirit of the times was the Million Man March being planned by Louis Farrakhan of the Nation of Islam and others. The idea had grown out of a National Black Leadership Summit held in June 1994. It was Farrakhan's idea, but other leaders, among them Jesse Jackson, liked it. African-American men, they said, were the most "endangered species" in America. The Million Man March would be a way for black men to show that they were aware of their own responsibility for their lives. Another purpose of the march was to assert that blacks could have political strength. This was the purpose that Jesse Jackson felt most comfortable supporting.

Much controversy surrounded the march: Women were being excluded; Farrakhan had a reputation as a hatemonger; and some people were concerned that the demonstration would turn violent. Still, the march took place on Monday, October 16, 1995. It did not attract a million men, but the participation of several hundred thousand men and their female supporters was impressive. The National Park Service estimated that four hundred thousand attended. A general air of peace and goodwill filled the crowd.

Jesse Jackson was among the speakers. He urged his listeners to use their political power—the power to vote: "What can a million men do? Eight million unregistered black voters. . . . The Gingrich forces won by nineteen thousand votes. They're cutting Medicaid; they're cutting Medicare; they're cutting scholarships; they're cutting legal assistance for women who are battered, victims of domestic violence. . . . Use your vote. We have the power to change the course."

The success of the Million Man March convinced Jesse Jackson that a new movement was possible. To his mind, a sleeping giant had been awakened and was beginning to stir. Jackson intended to guide that sleeping giant. One cause he believed in strongly was statehood for Washington, D.C., but that did not seem likely to happen. By 1995, the district was so financially troubled that Congress took over some of its operations. The question of statehood for the District of Columbia might not seriously arise again for years, so there was no chance of Jesse Jackson's campaigning to be its senator. By the end of 1995, Jackson had decided not to seek reelection as the district's "shadow senator." But he did not yet announce this decision to the public.

Coincidentally, also at the end of 1995, Jackson's son Jesse Jr. was elected to Congress. He would be the United States Representative from the Second Congressional District of Illinois. Jesse Jr. had been born on March 11, 1965, while his father was at the historic voting rights protest in Selma, Alabama. He grew up on the picket lines of the civil rights movement and spent his twenty-first birthday in a Washington, D.C., jail for taking part in a protest at the South African Embassy against apartheid. Most recently, he had served as the national field director of the National Rainbow Coalition. In this role, he had started a program that registered millions of new voters. He knew that he was closely identified with his father, but he intended to forge his own identity. He also showed pride in his father's accomplishments. Displayed in his congressional office was a life-size poster of Michael Jordan, the Chicago Bulls basketball team star, with a picture of his father's head pasted over Jordan's. "He's the Michael Jordan of what he does," said Jesse Jr. of his father.

With a son now on Capitol Hill, Jesse Jackson, Sr., turned his attention to a new movement for political and economic equality. He believed the time was ripe for this cause. In the middle of 1996, Jackson announced that he would not seek reelection as nonvoting "shadow senator" from Washington, D.C. He and his wife, Jacqueline, moved back to Chicago. There Jackson merged Operation PUSH with the National Rainbow Coalition, calling the organization the Rainbow/PUSH Coalition.

With Rainbow/PUSH, Jackson worked toward a variety of political and economic goals. On the political front, he renewed his calls for blacks to register to vote, warning that they were not using their potential political power. In June 1996, he and Chicago public school officials announced a new voting drive, called Reclaim Our Youth Teen Voter Registration Crusade. He also fought against the growing movement to end special treatment for minorities and women, particularly in higher education. When Proposition 209, which aimed to end affirmative action, was placed on the ballot in California, Jesse traveled to that state several times to campaign against it. On August 27, 1997, after the majority of voters had cast their ballots for the proposition, he led a protest march across the Golden Gate Bridge. The following February, he led another march in Los Angeles, calling it the Save the Dream March–California. Some Californians criticized him as an outsider trying to meddle in their affairs and called him a "carpetbagger." That was the nickname used during the post–Civil War Reconstruction period to describe northerners who went south for political or financial advantage.

In the economic arena, Jesse began a new campaign to fight discrimination in corporate America. In December 1996, in Cincinnati, Ohio, he called upon United Dairy Farmers to end discrimination against blacks on the part of its employees by January 15, 1997. If not, he said, the 207-store chain would face a boycott. Also in late 1996, he held a press conference and raised concerns about problems in the minority dealer development program operated by General Motors, the automobile manufacturer. Meetings with GM officials followed, and as a result, the GM program was reviewed by a Washington, D.C., law firm.

On January 15, 1997, the anniversary of Dr. Martin Luther King, Jr.'s birthday, Jackson announced the opening of a Rainbow/PUSH office on Wall Street. This New York City office would monitor opportunities for minorities in the nation's businesses. It would also educate minorities about job opportunities. Days later, Jackson announced the opening of an office in Detroit, Michigan, to push for more minority auto dealers, suppliers, and industry executives. Jackson wanted to see automobile manufacturers do more advertising in black media, stating that three Japanese automakers—Toyota, Mazda, and Subaru—had not spent a single dollar in advertising in black-owned newspapers during 1996.

Jackson kept a watchful eye on the entertainment business, too. In October 1997, a PolyGram executive said that if record companies were barred from hiring people with criminal records, no blacks would be working in the music industry. The Dutch-owned company removed the executive from his position and apologized for his statement, but Jackson believed that this sort of bigotry was all too common in the industry. Rainbow/PUSH bought stock in five entertainment companies. By owning stock, representatives of Rainbow/PUSH would be able to attend shareholders' meetings and obtain information on the companies' diversity programs. They could assess the hiring of women and minorities.

Although many reporters continued to express doubts about Jackson's activities, he remained a force to be reckoned with. Liberal Democrats understood that Jackson had many supporters, particularly among African Americans. Politicians who ignored or criticized Jackson risked losing the votes of his followers. Some people made cynical statements about Jackson, but others called him "the conscience of the nation." Both Jesse Jackson and Jesse Jr. were invited to speak at the Democratic National Convention in the summer of 1996. There President Bill Clinton was named as the Democratic candidate for the upcoming November election. Jesse Jackson began his speech by saying, "To my son, with whom I'm well pleased. . . ."

Clinton—the president most comfortable with blacks since Jimmy Carter—often asked Jackson for political advice. President Clinton came to consider Jackson a friend. Aware of Jackson's experience in diplomacy and mediation around the world, Clinton had asked him to lead a team of United States observers to South Africa's first post-apartheid elections in 1994. In 1996, Jesse served as coleader of a U.S. delegation to the fourth African/African-American Summit in Harare, Zimbabwe. In Clinton's second term as president, his administration took a new attitude toward Africa. It saw the potential of African nations as trade partners rather than as political pawns or international charity cases. The president turned to Jackson for help in pursuing this idea. In late 1997, the president named Jackson to the unpaid post of special U.S. envoy for the promotion of democracy in Africa. He was sworn in on October 10 by Secretary of State Madeleine Albright.

Jackson was eager to serve in this official capacity. He knew that Africa was a continent of great resources. But for those resources to be developed for the good of its people, he believed, democracy must flourish. And it must include a commitment to human rights and freedom of speech for the press. Less than two months later, Jackson made his first trip to Africa as the president's special envoy. He visited Kenya and Zambia, two nations with extensive, although imperfect, democratic records. Jackson met with government and opposition leaders in both countries. The following week, Secretary of State Madeleine Albright also visited Africa, holding talks in Ethiopia, Rwanda, Uganda, the Democratic Republic of Congo, South Africa, and Zimbabwe.

Barely a month after Jackson's African trip, he took

In 1997, as President Bill Clinton's special envoy to promote democracy in Africa, Jesse Jackson met with African leaders. Above, Jackson speaks with President Daniel Arap Moi of Kenya.

the opportunity to serve the president in another way. In January 1998, a scandal broke when reports surfaced of an alleged affair between Clinton and a former White House intern, twenty-four-year-old Monica Lewinsky. Jackson had become a friend of the Clinton family and was particularly concerned that the president's daughter would have difficulty weathering the firestorm surrounding her father. He telephoned Chelsea, a student at Stanford University in California, to lend moral support. Shortly afterward, the president invited Jackson to watch the Super Bowl with him on January 25. As the scandal grew, Jackson was often with the Clintons. In August, he joined them for a weekend at the presidential retreat at Camp David, Maryland. He prayed with them as the president prepared to address the nation. In his speech, President Clinton apologized for not having been entirely truthful about his relationship with the young woman. Said Jackson, "Sex is not the one string on the guitar. There are nine more Commandments." Political columnist Maureen Dowd referred to him as the "spiritual adviser" and as "the ambulance chaser of American politics."

In the meantime, Jackson continued his missions to Africa, accompanying the president on a trip there in March. He had two causes now—advising his friend the president, and helping the Mother Country, as he often called Africa.

It also seemed that he had not let go of his long-held dream of being the first African-American president or vice president of the United States. During 1997, Jackson spent a great deal of time in Iowa, which was not a state he usually visited. The earliest presidential primary election is held in Iowa. In October of that year, the *Chicago Tribune* reported that Jackson had been in Iowa more often than Vice President Al Gore, who was sure to seek the presidency in the year 2000. Jackson was there more than Senator Richard Gephardt, too, another likely candidate for the Democratic presidential nomination. In spite of his busy schedule, Jackson also managed to visit Iowa frequently in 1998. He was testing the waters and had no need to commit himself for at least a year.

In March 1999, though, Jackson decided not to seek the presidential bid. He said that he would instead concentrate on his efforts outside government, such as pushing Wall Street to support more minority businesses. "We intend to impact public policy in a major way in 1999 and 2000," said Jackson.

He continued his international diplomacy as well, traveling to Belgrade in April, where he successfully negotiated with Yugoslav president Slobodan Milosevic for the release of three U.S. soldiers captured during the Kosovo war.

"Carpetbagger?" "Ambulance chaser of American politics?" "Conscience of the nation?" Whatever one's opinion of Jesse Louis Jackson, Sr., no one can disagree that he is "somebody." He is somebody who had and continues to have a dream. He dreams of a better country and a better world—and of himself as a leader in the realization of that dream. But Jackson also understands that he might not achieve his dream. As he has said, "A dream is not just an end result, a dream is also a process. I feel the job is being a participant in the process."

CHRONOLOGY

1941—Born October 8 in Greenville, South Carolina.

1950—Nine-year-old Jesse gives his first public speech at a church Christmas pageant.

1955—Enters Sterling High School and signs up for football, basketball, and baseball.

1959—Graduates from high school; enters the University of Illinois in Chicago.

1960—Transfers to Agricultural and Technical College of North Carolina at Greensboro; begins activism for civil rights.

1962—Marries Jacqueline Lavinia Brown on December 31.

1964—Graduates from college; moves to Chicago and enrolls in Chicago Theological Seminary.

1965—Participates in civil rights march led by Dr. Martin Luther King, Jr., in Selma, Alabama.

1966—Leaves seminary; joins staff of Martin Luther King's Southern Christian Leadership Conference (SCLC) as head of Operation Breadbasket, trying to create jobs for blacks and help black-owned businesses.

1967—Becomes national director of Operation Breadbasket.

1968—Accompanies Dr. King and SCLC leaders to Memphis, Tennessee, where King is assassinated on April 4; Jesse is ordained as a minister.

1969—Is granted an honorary degree by Chicago Theological Seminary.

1970—Leads a march in Washington, D.C., to commemorate Dr. King.

1971—Runs unsuccessfully for mayor of Chicago; stages the Black Expo; travels to Nigeria on a cultural exchange; resigns from SCLC and announces formation of Operation PUSH (People United to Save Humanity) to help improve economic status of blacks.

1975—Starts PUSH EXCEL (push for excellence) and travels around the country on a lecture tour to inspire teens to succeed in school.

1979—Travels to Middle East and meets with Arab leaders in an unsuccessful attempt to improve in Arab-Israeli relations.

1983—Representing minorities and disadvantaged groups—which he calls the "Rainbow Coalition"—enters the race to become the Democratic candidate for president of the United States; negotiates the release of Lieutenant Robert Goodman, Jr., who was being held hostage in Syria.

1984—Does not win the presidential nomination; founds the National Rainbow Coalition.

1985—Leads a reenactment of Martin Luther King's 1965 march in Selma, Alabama.

1986—Announces a new National Rainbow Coalition—an organization for social justice that would be a "progressive force" in the Democratic Party.

1987—Declares himself a presidential candidate for the 1988 Democratic nomination.

1988—Gains strong support but does not win the presidential nomination.

1989—Is awarded the Spingarn Medal, an annual award by the National Association for the Advancement of Colored People (NAACP) to honor the person with the highest achievement in his or her field.

1990—Meets with Nelson Mandela, the anti-apartheid leader, in South Africa and with Iraqi leader Saddam Hussein; television show premieres in October; campaigns to be elected "shadow senator" of Washington, D.C., a nonvoting member of the Senate.

1991—Sworn in as "shadow senator" and lobbies to make Washington, D.C., a state; U.S. Postal Service issues a Jesse Jackson pictorial cancellation.

1992—Hosts a new television show, *Both Sides With Jesse Jackson*, on CNN.

1994—Leads a team of United States observers to South Africa's first post-apartheid elections.

1995—Speaks at the Million Man March in Washington, D.C.

1996—Serves as coleader of a United States delegation to the fourth African/African-American Summit in Harare, Zimbabwe; merges Operation PUSH with the National Rainbow Coalition, calling it the Rainbow/PUSH Coalition.

1997—Sworn in as special United States envoy for the promotion of democracy in Africa.

1998—Continues diplomacy in support of democratic reforms in Kenya.

1999—Successfully negotiates the release of three U.S. prisoners in Yugoslavia during the war in Kosovo.

BIBLIOGRAPHY

Books

Barker, Lucius J. *Our Time Has Come*. Urbana. Ill.: University of Illinois Press, 1988.

————, and Ronald W. Walters, eds. *Jesse Jackson's 1984 Presidential Campaign*. Urbana, Ill.: University of Illinois Press, 1989.

Chaplik, Dorothy. *Up With Hope: A Biography of Jesse Jackson*. Minneapolis, Minn.: Dillon Press, 1986.

Faw, Bob, and Nancy Skelton. *Thunder in America: The Improbable Presidential Campaign of Jesse Jackson*. Austin, Tex.: Texas Monthly Press, 1986.

Frady, Marshall. *Jesse: The Life and Pilgrimage of Jesse Jackson*. New York: Random House, 1996

Haskins, James. *The Life and Death of Martin Luther King, Jr.* New York: Lothrop, Lee & Shepard, 1977.

Jackson, Jesse. *A Time to Speak: The Autobiography of the Reverend Jesse Jackson*. New York: Simon & Schuster, 1988.

Kosof, Anna. *Jesse Jackson*. New York: Franklin Watts, 1987.

Landess, Thomas, and Richard Quinn. *Jesse Jackson and the Politics of Race*. Ottawa, Ill.: Jameson Books, 1985.

McKissack, Patricia C. *Jesse Jackson: A Biography*. New York: Scholastic, Inc., 1989.

Otfinoski, Steven. *Jesse Jackson, A Voice for Change*. New York: Fawcett Columbine, 1989.

Reed, Adolph L., Jr. *The Jesse Jackson Phenomenon*. New Haven, Conn.: Yale University Press, 1986.

Reynolds, Barbara A. *Jesse Jackson: The Man, the Movement, the Myth*. Chicago: Nelson-Hall, 1975.

Stone, Eddie. *Jesse Jackson*. Los Angeles: Holloway House, 1979.

Westman, Paul. *Jesse Jackson, I Am Somebody*. Minneapolis, Minn.: Dillon Press, 1981.

Wilkinson, Brenda. *Jesse Jackson: Still Fighting for the Dream*. Englewood Cliffs, N.J.: Silver Burdett Press, Inc., 1990.

Articles

Anderson, Kurt. "Jackson Plays By the Rules: A Good Soldier—But Drafting His Own Battle Plan." *Time*, November 5, 1984, p. 29.

Barrat, Laurence L. "Ready to Play Ball." *Time*, June 20, 1988, pp. 12–13.

"Behind the Hero, Black History." Editorial. *The New York Times*, July 22, 1988, p. A30.

Booker, Simeon. "Jackson Brings Blacks' Political Aspirations to Spotlight at Convention," *Jet*. August 1, 1988, pp. 4–8.

Burns. John F. "Security Tight for Jackson On Arrival in South Africa." *The New York Times*, February 8, 1990, p. A18.

Cheers, D. Michael. "Jackson's Southern Strategy Highlights Service to Region." *Jet*, March 7, 1988, pp. 4–8.

———. "Southern Blacks Rally to Give Jackson First Wins in Presidential Primaries." *Jet*, March 28, 1988, pp. 4–9.

Davis, Peter, and Martin Ames. "The Two-Ring Circus and the White Man's Ball." *Esquire*, November 1988, pp. 125–131.

Dionne, E. J., Jr. "New Split on Jackson Hostage Offer." *The New York Times*, July 30, 1988, p. 1.

Dowd, Maureen. "Looking to '92." *The New York Times*, February 28, 1990, p. A20.

———. "Jesse Jackson Helps President Deal with Lewinsky Allegations," *New York Times News Service*, March 27, 1998.

Goodman, Walter, "Jackson on Assignment in Iraq: Reporter Becomes the Story." *The New York Times*, September 5, 1990, p. C13.

"I'm Not Angry; We'll Keep the Dream Alive." *USA Today*, July 13, 1988, p. 11A.

"Jackson and the Jews." Editorial. *The New Republic*, March 19, 1984, p. 9.

"Jackson Leaves for Moscow; Hopes to Aid Armenia Victims," *The New York Times*, January 29, 1989, p. 15.

"Jesse Comes Calling." *Time*, February 19, 1990, p. 44.

Johnson, Dick. "Jackson's Refusal to Back Daley Angers Some in Party." *The New York Times*, March 6, 1989, p. B10.

Kantrowitz. Barbara, and Karen Springen. "Black and White in America." *Newsweek*, March 7, 1988, pp. 18–25.

King, Wayne. "Man Charged in Plot on Jackson Suggested Others Were Involved." *The New York Times*, May 19, 1988, pp. Al, B12.

Klein, Joe. "Jesse Jackson for President?" *New York*, April 11, 1988, pp. 24, 26–27.

"Mandela Expects to Be Released Soon, His Wife Says." *The New York Times*, January 9, 1990, p. A3.

Martz, Larry, et al. "The Power Broker." *Newsweek*, March 21, 1988, pp. 18–22.

Meyer, Peter, and Stephanie Siewka. "Poll Power: Jesse Jackson's Surge Is Launching a New Generation of Black Leaders." *Life*, Spring 1988, pp. 34–38.

McQuiston, John T. "Missouri Couple Held On Charges of Plotting to Assassinate Jackson." *The New York Times*, May 19, 1988, pp. Al, D30.

"The New Gospel According to PUSH." *Newsweek*, August 16, 1982, p. 52.

O'Connor, John J. "Jesse Jackson Finds a Platform on a Sitcom." *The New York Times*, April 27, 1989, p. C28.

Oreskes, Michael. "Gerald Austin Provides Direction and Order to Jackson's Candidacy." *The New York Times*, May 6, 1988, p. A18.

———. "Jackson Wants Chance for No. 2 Spot." *The New York Times*, June 7, 1988, p. 10.

———. "Jackson 'Too Mature' for Anger, Icily Offers No Embrace for Ticket." *The New York Times*, July 12, 1988, pp. Al, A17.

———. "Voters and Jackson: Confronting Racial Limitations and Lifting Them, A Bit." *The New York Times*, August 13, 1988. p. 9.

Orin, Deborah, "It's Getting Personal." *New York Post*, March 31, 1988, p. 4.

Plattner, Andy, et al. "The Preacher and His Programs." *U.S. News and World Report*, April 11, 1988, pp. 30–33.

Purnick, Joyce, and Michael Oreskes. "Jesse Jackson Aims for the Mainstream." *The New York Times Magazine*, November 29, 1987, pp. 23ff.

Rhodes, John. "Campaign '88: Dems on the Issues." *New York Daily News*, April 17, 1988, pp. 6–7.

Rosenthal, Andrew. "Jackson Preaches to Large Crowds in Colorado on Eve of Party Caucuses." *The New York Times*, April 4, 1988, p. 10.

———. Letter By Jackson Hints at a Shift." *The New York Times*, March 7, 1989, p. 10.

Shapiro, Walter. "Win, Jesse, Win." *Time*, April 4, 1988, p. 21.

Smothers, Ronald. "The Impact of Jesse Jackson." *The New York Times Magazine*, March 4, 1984, p. 40ff.

———. "Why the Higher Rungs of Power Elude Black Politicians." *The New York Times*, February 26, 1989, p. 1.

"What Makes Jesse Run." *The Sunday Times Magazine* (London), March 27, 1988, pp. 20–36.

Weinraub, Bernard. "Jackson's Income Exceeded $200,000." *The New York Times*, May 4, 1988, p. B8.

Zoglin. Richard. "Keeping All Kinds of Hope Alive." *Time*, October 1, 1990, p. 82.

Television Programs

The MacNeil-Lehrer NewsHour, PBS, October 16, 1995.

Frontline, PBS, April 30, 1996.

Internet Addresses

<http://www.pbs.org/wgbh/pages/frontline/jesse/>

<http://www.rainbowpush.org/jjackson/jj.html>

INDEX